LEAVE OF ABSENCE

OTHER PLAYS BY
LUCIA FRANGIONE

Cariboo Magi *
Chickens
Christmas on the Air
Cinderella
Espresso *
Frankie Armitage
FRESCO
Holy Mo
Maid for a Musket
Maybe Mary
Mistletoads
MMM
Paradise Garden *
Wobbling Madonna

* Published by Talonbooks

LEAVE OF ABSENCE

Lucia Frangione

with songs by Jim Hodgkinson

TALONBOOKS

© 2013 by Lucia Frangione

Talonbooks
P.O. Box 2076, Vancouver, British Columbia V6B 3S3
www.talonbooks.com

Typeset in Frutiger Serif
Printed and bound in Canada on 100% post-consumer recycled paper.
Typeset by Typesmith. Cover illustration by Emily Cooper.

First printing: 2013

The publisher gratefully acknowledges the financial support of the Canada Council for the Arts, the Government of Canada through the Canada Book Fund, and the Province of British Columbia through the British Columbia Arts Council and the Book Publishing Tax Credit for our publishing activities.

Rights to produce *Leave of Absence*, in whole or in part, in any medium by any group, amateur or professional, are retained by the author. Interested persons are requested to contact Catherine Knights, Catalyst Talent Creative Management, email catherine@catalysttcm.com or telephone 416-645-0935.

LIBRARY AND ARCHIVES CANADA CATALOGUING IN PUBLICATION

Frangione, Lucia
    Leave of absence / Lucia Frangione.

A play.
Issued also in electronic format.
ISBN 978-0-88922-753-8

    I. Title.

PS8561.R27755L43 2013   C812'.54   C2012-908094-2

For Father Rob Repicky,
Michael Kopsa,
and Dr. Michael Davenport

– three inspiring and present fathers

FOREWORD

Leave of Absence is a complex story that forces the reader out of the black and white and into the grey of life. And like most thought-provoking and visceral writing, it is filled with paradox.

Lucia Frangione is a writer who is not afraid to live in the uneasy place of paradox. Her authentic voice delivers validity to points of view that don't often share the same page. She illustrates the sacred in what to many readers seems profane. She pinpoints the soul-journey of the individual within the context of community. She understands love in people many would deem to be unlovable.

Frangione's work is inspired by primal expressions of humanity while reaching for transcendence. She is a writer of rare spirit, driven by the need to articulate the cravings of the soul within limitations of our everyday experience. What happens when day-to-day existence renders the soul hollow? How do people of principle find their spiritual and communal mooring in such a place? This play explores these questions through scenes rooted in primal acts of innocent curiosity, violence, communal upheaval, and love.

There is nothing more wonderful than a story that reveals complex humanity. *Leave of Absence* is such a story.

> – MORRIS ERTMAN
> Director

PREFACE

Most of us would say we have done nothing purposefully to cause a child harm. We read about Amanda Todd or Jamie Hubley in the news and can't even imagine participating in such horrific persecution. How does this even happen in our society and why are children killing each other or themselves? I had washed my own hands clean all my life until I started asking myself: What have I *not* done to protect a child? How have I have been absent?

This play is about a small, loving community who all, in their own way, help raise a child. It's full of humour, sensuality, and mysticism. It contains some of my experiences as a fourteen-year-old girl, including some of my prayer poetry from that time. It was inspired originally by the experiences my friend Rob Repicky shared with me: being a priest in Toronto for more than twenty years. But the play also goes to a place I've never gone before. It is my own leave – of absence.

Every year children and young adults looking for a person to talk to find me through Facebook (social media can also do some good). Why me? My God, I don't know. I'm entirely unqualified. But I guess I am unafraid to ask questions about faith and sexuality in my work, so that's a start. They pour out their anguish over being bullied, excluded, or shamed by others and by the voice in their own head.

Many of them are from a religious community, so the threat isn't just emotional and physical but also spiritual. Some of these kids and adults haven't yet been sexually active. Almost all confess they have tried to kill themselves or feel they may someday. We have conversations that last for years sometimes. Some lose their faith. I've seen others become sexually inert – for decades. Still others are able to hold on to a faith while living and loving as someone other than straight.

When John Patrick Shanley was asked why he left the question of Father Flynn's innocence open in his play *Doubt*, he wrote: "What I'm not interested in is writing polemics on one side of an issue or another. Doubt does not have to dismantle passion. It can be a passionate exercise."

In *Leave of Absence*, I share with you five people. I share with you five different viewpoints. I share with you five different ways to love. Within this, I ask the questions: Where is the absence? How does a child slip through our hands?

The answer to these questions, only you know for your life. And in asking them, I do what I can to catch a child from falling.

– LUCIA FRANGIONE
December 9, 2012

ACKNOWLEDGEMENTS

This play was developed with the support of the Canada Council for the Arts, the Gordon Armstrong Playwright's Rent Award, Pacific Theatre, David McFazdean and family, Playwrights Theatre Centre, Alberta Theatre Projects, and Lamb's Players Theatre (San Diego). Many thanks to Rob Repicky for sharing his experiences as a priest. Thank you also to Michael Kopsa for inspiring me to write this play and to physicist Dr. Michael Davenport for the insight into science and the spiritual. Special thanks to D. D. Kugler, my dramaturge, and to ACTivist Theatre Collective, who produced a thirty-minute version of the script at the Vancouver International Fringe Festival in September 2011.

PRODUCTION HISTORY

Leave of Absence premiered at Pacific Theatre in Vancouver, British Columbia, on January 25, 2013, with the following cast:

FATHER RYAN: Tom McBeath

BLAKE: Karyn Guenther

GRETA: Lucia Frangione

MARTHA (MISS WOODS): Marie Russell

LEAP (FILIPP): Craig Erickson

Artistic direction by Ron Reed
Produced by Alison Chisholm
Publicity by Andrea Loewen
Production management by Frank Nickel
Technical direction by Jessica Howell

Directed by Morris Ertman
Dramaturgy by D. D. Kugler
Stage managed by Jethelo E. Cabilete

Set designed by Drew Facey
Lighting designed by Lauchlin Johnston
Sound designed by Jeff Tymoschuk and Jim Hodgkinson
Properties managed by Linsy Rotar
Costumes designed by Sydney Cavanagh

THE COMMUNITY

RYAN:
Late fifties, a Roman Catholic priest, a quiet, thinking, and gentle man.

GRETA:
Late thirties, single mom, counsellor at a women's shelter, a provocateur.

LEAP (FILIPP):
Forty, Russian, a former boxer, does construction, physically immaculate.

MARTHA (MISS WOODS):
Early fifties, school principal and church worship leader, an ageless, modest, plain woman with an intimate, beautiful, and utterly sincere faith.

BLAKE:
Fifteen, Greta's daughter, awkward as a newborn calf, utterly transparent.

THE TIME AND PLACE
The present. Several locations within a booming bedroom community outside a large Canadian city.

PERFORMANCE NOTE

production note ✱

This play is very much about community. We may feel we are speaking, acting, and loving in isolation, but what we do affects others. What we don't do affects others. And sometimes a memory will feel so strong, it enters the room. In the staging of Leave of Absence, moments in isolated spaces overlap one by one and often play out together within the same scene. The characters within one scene may create an isolated space: a circle, if you will. But that circle often overlaps with another circle. A character can have two realities going on at once if he or she is standing in the place where the circles overlap.

LEAVE OF
ABSENCE

ACT ONE

SCENE ONE

BLAKE has just burst into Father RYAN's office for counselling.

BLAKE:
Why am I in trouble? I punched Tracy in the face. She has a black eye. But she punched me first.

BLAKE rolls up her sleeve and shows a deeply bruised arm, enough to worry about.

RYAN:
Whoa.

BLAKE:
I shouldn't have hit her back. Okay? She's only fourteen, I'm fifteen. "It's not what Jesus would do." Can I go?

RYAN:
Hold on. So ... Tracy's your friend?

BLAKE:
Best friend. Was.

RYAN:
What changed?

BLAKE crosses her arms over her chest.

BLAKE:
This summer. Boom. She grew a full rack. School starts and now the boys want to get it on with her and the popular girls hang around for sloppy seconds behind the skating rink. "Come on, Blake, I know you're flat but if you let them in your pants you could be cool." But I'm not into it. So, yesterday,

suddenly she won't talk to me in the hallway and she's Chantel's partner in gym class. And today she punches me at recess to show off. But then later she sticks this in my locker (*pulls out a little note with a bright friendly doodling of penguins*): "You're still my best friend. You still know me like nobody else." We've been drawing these penguins since grade two ...

> *BLAKE starts to tear up. RYAN offers her a tissue.*
> *She waves it off.*

BLAKE:
 I'm cool.

RYAN:
 I admire your integrity. You didn't let the loss of her friendship compromise what you believe in.

BLAKE:
 You just don't want me having sex. That's all.

RYAN:
 That's not what I said.

BLAKE:
 She can be nice too.

RYAN:
 Yeah?

BLAKE:
 And funny. Once, in the girl's washroom, Julie Marshall went in to pee, right? And Tracy sat in the stall next to her, like confession, and spoke through the toilet-roll dispenser: "What are your sins, my child?" And poor Julie had to confess before we gave her any paper.

RYAN:
 (*smiles*) Uh-huh.

BLAKE:
Then I said, "Say three Hail Marys and wipe front to back ..."
And Tracy laughed so hard she peed her own pants.

RYAN:
(*smiles*) Funny.

BLAKE:
So, if I'm not in trouble, why did you ask to see me?

RYAN:
You don't strike me as the violent type.

BLAKE:
You don't know me.

RYAN:
That's why I want to see you. I've enjoyed our chats in class.
I've seen you with your mom at church. But I haven't taken
the time to actually sit down with you one-on-one. I've
noticed in religious studies you've revised the Apostles'
Creed ...

BLAKE:
I'm not going to pray about something I don't believe.

RYAN:
I'd love to hear what you do believe.

BLAKE:
Don't be so sure.

    BLAKE grabs her bag and heads towards the door.

RYAN:
Try me.

    She smiles, slips away.

SCENE TWO

*The community of RYAN and BLAKE's world
opens up around them. Moments in isolated
spaces overlap one by one and play out together,
building to a cacophonous peak.*

*The first moment to overlap is MARTHA speaking
to the congregation.*

*MARTHA approaches the congregation as worship
leader. She holds her songbook reverently, as
though it were the Ark of the Covenant. She opens
it carefully.*

MARTHA:
Good morning, brothers and sisters. In keeping with our worship
focus on the female mystics of the thirteenth century, I wish to
share Saint Gertrude the Great of Helfta's Spiritual Exercises.

*She begins reverently to sing "Daybreak." As
the mystical and sensual words start to hit the
congregation, teenaged boys begin to snicker and
then laugh out loud. MARTHA becomes conscious
of the fact that they are reducing the words to
vulgarity. Despite her shock and embarrassment,
she finishes the song with as much pained dignity
as she can muster without crying.*

(*singing*)

For you I watch at daybreak.
For you my soul has thirsted,
For you my flesh.

Visit me now in the morning at daybreak ...
Come to me now bountifully
That I might
Dulcetly melt into you ...

When will you satisfy me with yourself?
If only I might here perceive
The fine rays
Of your Venus-like beauty.

For a little while and at least
Be permitted to anticipate
Your gentleness
For a short time and pleasantly
Beforehand to taste you.

If only
I were granted to come.
To come taste you
If only
I were granted to come.

So Sexual

*A second moment overlaps. BLAKE is on the bus,
faintly reciting to herself her own version of the
Apostles' Creed, a little pleased RYAN had noticed
her personal version.*

BLAKE:
I believe in God the Father (and/or Mother),
the Almighty,
maker of heaven and earth,
the Higgs boson, and the big bang.

gender equality-

And in Jesus Christ,
his or her only begotten Son, our Lord,
who was conceived by the Holy Ghost;
born of the Virgin Mary
(though not necessarily a virgin);
suffered under Pontius Pilate;
was crucified, died, and was buried.
He descended into hell
(which is probably a state of mind not a physical place).
On the third day, he rose again from the dead
(maybe a metaphor).

He ascended into heaven
(the collective unconscious),
and sits at the right hand of God the Father (and/or
Mother) Almighty.
From thence he shall come to judge the quick and the dead.

I believe in the Holy Ghost;

I believe in the not-so-holy Roman Catholic Church
(and the Pope is not infallible);
the communion of saints;
the forgiveness of sins;
the resurrection (or recycling) of the body;
and the life everlasting.

Amen.

*A third moment. LEAP is in his garage. He has
hung a punching bag from the rafters and is
boxing with bare, bloody fists, his gloves thrown
on the floor beside him. He wears jogging pants,
no shirt, sweat glistening on his bare chest. A gold
cross flashes around his neck.*

*A fourth moment. The garden outside LEAP's
garage. RYAN, wearing his clerical collar, strokes
hair away from the face of a dead woman, SONJA,
lying in the grass. He closes her eyes, makes the
sign of the cross, and begins the sacrament of the
Anointing of the Sick. He prays for her.*

RYAN:
Be strong, do not fear; your God will come.
The desert and the parched land will be glad;
the wilderness will rejoice and blossom.
Like the crocus, it will burst into bloom ...

RYAN continues praying over her in hushed tones

and then he anoints her forehead and hands with blessed oil and quietly reads the Bible to her.

A fifth moment. GRETA soberly yanks a For Sale sign out of her front yard. She kicks the uprooted sod back with her high heels.

GRETA:
Home.

Her phone rings. She answers.

GRETA:
Hello, Greta here. (*hears of SONJA's death*) What ...? What?! Oh my God ...

The overlapping music and sounds of the scenes – the sound of BLAKE's bus coming to a halt and the swarming of bees – rise in volume. Then, suddenly, silence. GRETA puts away her phone. MARTHA gathers her music. BLAKE, carrying her school bag, enters GRETA's house. LEAP crumples to the floor. RYAN kisses SONJA's hand. He was close to her.

RYAN:
Sonja ...

BLAKE and GRETA are in the new house. GRETA has her shoes off.

GRETA:
You get lost?

BLAKE:
No. It's two buses.

GRETA:
You know Sonja from church?

BLAKE:
Married to the Russian?

GRETA:
Yeah. She just died.

BLAKE:
What?!

GRETA:
It must have happened fast. Leap came back from his run ...
the door was wide open, the dog going wild, dragging him into
the backyard ...

BLAKE:
No ...

GRETA:
He found her in the flower bed, puffed up like a balloon. Ants
crawling into her nose.

BLAKE:
(*wincing*) Mom.

GRETA:
Bee-sting. Stupid way to die. (*kisses her daughter on the head*)
We're all so fragile.

BLAKE:
Yeah.

GRETA invites BLAKE into their new home.

GRETA:
Take off your boots – hardwood floors.

*BLAKE kicks off her boots and GRETA moves into
the space of the new house.*

SCENE THREE

*RYAN carefully approaches LEAP and sits on the
floor beside him.*

RYAN:
(*to LEAP*) When somebody I love dies, I set aside the clerical
collar for a minute and return to physics. I think of the space
between particles, the molecules that don't disappear with
death but reconfigure. I think of the dancing enzymes that
keep cells alive. When the priest in me can't quite fathom
resurrection, the scientist in me can. Some may say physics is
cold and calculated ... well ... it is calculated ... but it's far from
cold.

*RYAN walks over to SONJA. LEAP does not follow,
but listens.*

LEAP:
I wish you could recalculate her back.

RYAN:
Me too. But it comforts me to know Sonja's entangled with
everything alive: from the elegant symmetries of a quark to
the astonishing energy of a quasar. She entangled with you.
With me.

LEAP:
Wishful thinking.

*RYAN kisses SONJA's exposed palm, then lifts her
hand and places it across her heart.*

RYAN:
Quantum mechanics. The transactional interpretation. Our present reality is a negotiation between our past and our future. Or as Saint Augustine would say: God creates with all time.

LEAP:
I didn't get to Sonja in time. That's all I know. She is not here. She is lost to us.

RYAN:
There is great mystery, Leap. I can't imagine your grief. Sonja is not "here," but I do believe Sonja is "there." If that's any hope. Being mortal, we only live on one side of the equal sign. We can't see the entire equation yet.

same for those who oppose equality?

LEAP:
Or maybe God just isn't very good with math.

SCENE FOUR

GRETA is touring BLAKE through the new house.

GRETA:
I can't believe this place is ours! The oak staircase. Look, it still has the original mouldings ...!

BLAKE:
You remember I got piano at five, right?

GRETA:
Did you see the view?!

BLAKE peeks at it.

BLAKE:
That lawn is going to be a bitch to mow.

GRETA:
That's what I love about you, Blake. Your gratefulness. Did you see your bedroom has a dormer right over the cherry tree?

BLAKE:
I'm gonna fit right in with all these BMWs and poodle dogs ...   *not*

GRETA:
Man. I can't win with you. When we lived in the duplex you said you were too embarrassed to bring friends over because we didn't have a "real" house.

BLAKE:
I didn't mean that ...

GRETA:
Do you know how hard it is to buy a home as a single mom? I'm a freakin' superhero here and you can't even say thank you?!

BLAKE:
I'm just saying I liked our old place!

GRETA:
You liked being three blocks away from Tracy! Well, if she's really your friend, she can hop on her bike.

LEAP half-heartedly flips through a selection of sheet music. MARTHA enters with more.

LEAP:
You pick the music, Martha. She always liked your voice.

MARTHA gives LEAP a great big tearful hug.

MARTHA:
We'll miss her in the choir. She sang like a little sparrow. Oh,
Leap. I'm so sorry.

LEAP:
Yeah.

MARTHA:
She was a dear friend.

MARTHA mops up her nose, then offers a hymn.

MARTHA:
How about "We Shall Sleep But Not Forever." It has this lovely
verse about gardening ...

(*singing gently*)

When we see a precious blossom
That we tended with such care
Rudely taken from our bosom
How our aching hearts despair ...

LEAP:
Okay. Just, no song about Jesus "coming coming."

MARTHA:
Well, I ... I didn't mean it quite like that ...

LEAP:
I know.

MARTHA:
The song is about reuniting with Jesus. Imagine where Sonja
is right now.

LEAP:
She's in a cardboard box.

MARTHA:
I mean, her spirit.

LEAP sighs, closes the music book, and hands it back to her.

MARTHA:
Sometimes I yearn for heaven. Not that I don't love life here. But I ache to return to the place I used to belong. Like wanting to go back to the old farm long after it's been sold. Sonja is lucky. She's truly home.

LEAP:
She's dead.

MARTHA:
Death feels unnatural to me. Like we've been robbed. But of course death is completely natural. So is aging but, goodness gracious, I hate getting arthritis in my fingers. I want to be immortal. I want my loved ones to never die.

LEAP:
Yeah, well ...

MARTHA:
I think we're not built for death, we're built for eternity. And our natural state is love and perfect beauty. And someday we'll have it. But right now ... we do our best. Sometimes I wonder if I was a good-enough friend to Sonja ...

LEAP sighs. Stands.

LEAP:
Everyone was good to her. But why do we need to believe she's floating around somewhere? She's dead. And it's her own damn fault. That's it.

LEAP stands; he's done.

MARTHA:
I'm sorry ...

*He pulls SONJA's wedding ring out of his pocket
and holds it up to the light.*

LEAP:
When I bought this ring for Sonja, I never thought I'd have to
pawn it to pay for her coffin. heartbreaking.

SCENE FIVE

*GRETA opens RYAN's door, BLAKE in tow with her
headphones on.*

GRETA:
Wait there, Blake. I'll only be five minutes. (*shuts the door
behind her and turns to RYAN*) Hey. How's Leap doing? Poor
guy.

RYAN:
Surviving.

GRETA:
Let me know if I can help with the funeral.

RYAN:
Thanks.

GRETA:
I have some good news for a change.

RYAN:
What?

GRETA:
The phone drive brought in 260 jackets.

RYAN:

Really?! Fantastic! And they're not all size-seven pink parkas with a broken zipper?

GRETA:

No, pretty decent pickings. There's a black down-filled coat I'm dying to get on that skinny guy with the scabs.

RYAN:

Scott.

GRETA:

Really?

RYAN:

Now you'll never forget his name.

GRETA:

And we got a letter from Nardeep. Remember her from the shelter? About four years ago she came in with her head bashed open by a can of chicken-noodle soup?

RYAN:

"I'll never buy chunky style again. It hurts."

GRETA:

I think she's alive today because of her sense of humour. The hell that woman's been through.

survival tool

RYAN:

You called it. If you didn't approach her in the parking lot – (*opens the letter and looks at a photo, sees the writing on the back, pleased*) Hey, Nardeep is walking the Camino!

GRETA:

The what?

RYAN:

The Camino de Santiago. You start in France, walk through the

Basque region, and all across the north of Spain. I've always wanted to do it. But it takes about six weeks. I can't imagine being able to get away for that long.

GRETA leans in.

GRETA:
I think Martha's overreacting. Blake and Tracy are fighting, but they're teenagers. It's going to happen.

RYAN:
Martha just asked me to talk to her.

GRETA:
Yeah? Well, Martha called me in to the principal's office today to discuss Blake's unhealthy attachment to Tracy.

RYAN:
What does that mean?

GRETA:
She insinuated that Blake doesn't have a strong-enough sense of family because I'm a single mom. She relies too much on Tracy and needs to make more friends. Blake's always been an oddball. She's a late bloomer and Tracy's all about boys and parties. I think Martha's worried about the bad influence. I did catch Blake and Tracy doing a show-and-tell last week. A "Do you have what I have?" sort of thing.

RYAN:
Does Blake talk to you?

GRETA:
About puberty? Yeah, right up there with world economics. You kidding? I had the opposite problem: got my boobs early. Half a dozen guys would swarm me in the hallway, hornets with hands.

RYAN:

Can't win when you're a teenager.

GRETA:

Once I stayed home for three days because I got chased with a dental pick. They didn't call it sexual harassment back then, they called it being busty.

RYAN:

I went to a small private school. The worst we got there was a wedgie.

GRETA:

Were you popular? Must have been cute ...

RYAN:

I was a nerd. Long feathered hair. The seventies. And glasses. Thick.

GRETA:

Too bad I didn't know you back then. Probably would have steamed those Coke bottles up. *flirty*

RYAN:

I doubt it. When I was sixteen, you were still in diapers. (*sits behind his desk*) Blake's a great kid.

GRETA:

Yeah. She's smart, huh? But even Blake is going to be hit with the hormone madness of puberty. Doesn't Martha remember what that's like? Good God. When I'm ovulating, everything turns me on. And not just men! Women with large noses do it for me. Ice cream cones, the stick shift in the car. Once I saw my cat eating the ripped-out belly of a baby bird; I don't know what it was, the soft feathers, the absolute pleasure she had licking out the insides ... I couldn't stop thinking about it. My daughter discovering her body and how it works is titillating. I guess because she's a piece of me so I get to experience the

newness all over again. The miracle. I'm sure even you get a
little hot under the clerical collar.   *"appropiate?"*

RYAN:
Why would you say that?

GRETA:
There's no shame in having a primal response. It's what you
do with it. Sexuality is fluid, it can be influenced. It can be
channelled. Some can dam it up into the priesthood and wait
for it to evaporate.

> *RYAN just looks at her. Dangerous little moment.*

RYAN:
Some suck it up into a deep pool so they can wallow in it.

GRETA:
Wallow?

RYAN:
I mean your conversations, your humour. You dress
provocatively.

GRETA:
So?

RYAN:
Ever notice you talk about your cleavage when you're
nervous?

GRETA:
I talk about my breasts?!

RYAN:
All the time. Just now, you changed the conversation away
from your daughter's troubles and made it all about you being
busty.

GRETA:
Why would I do that?!

RYAN:
I don't know!

GRETA:
(*she pats them trying to figure it out*) They're always here for me.
(*holds them*) I hold them. When I'm anxious.

RYAN:
Yup.

GRETA:
(*smiles*) You noticed that too.

RYAN:
The priesthood isn't damming up my sexuality.   *Really?*

GRETA:
Don't lie to me, Ryan.

RYAN:
Honestly, I got to an age where the only thirty-year-old I was
dreaming about was a Scotch.

GRETA:
Uh-huh. You don't channel all your sexual energy into Scotch.
You constantly provoke a kind of intercourse with me. And
everyone can see it. You dare me to cross a line, I do, and then
you spank me. (*watches him*) And you like it.

RYAN:
No, *you* like it. (*pause*) Greta, you're one of my dearest friends.

GRETA:
And you're one of mine. Elliott asked me to marry him. Move
to Toronto. But I bought a house here instead. By myself.
There's a part of me that waits for you. And I think, "Oh, Greta,

it's just because you want what you can't have. You don't know the real man, you only know the priest." But I don't have a choice in this. (*no response*) I love you. (*no response*) You have nothing to say?

> GRETA *tears up, leaves him. As soon as he's alone,* RYAN *exhales, rubs his hands over his chest and neck as though he's wrestling out of a sensual embrace.*

> BLAKE *peeks into* RYAN's *office again.*

RYAN:
   Blake, hi!

BLAKE:
   Miss Woods said you wanted to see me again?

RYAN:
   Yes. Come on in. Can I get you a tea?

BLAKE:
   No. Thanks.

RYAN:
   How are things going this week? (*no response*) Miss Woods is a little concerned you're getting picked on.

BLAKE:
   (*blurts*) Everyone's calling me a lesbian but Tracy's the one with the sick "biology" DVD from her dad.

RYAN:
   What?

BLAKE:
You tell and I will die.

RYAN:
I won't tell.

BLAKE:
He sneaks Tracy a DVD cuz her mom's always snooping
through the Internet history. It's all men who have huge ...
you know. With schoolgirls on the desk and ... just ... everywhere. Gross. And girls with girls ... like cheerleaders ... really
close up. It's totally sick. _closet_

Tracy was pretending they were iffy but I knew she was into it.
God. She even asked me if I wanted to try stuff with her, you
know, for parties where you invite guys –

Anyway, I said, "Get out, no way!"

RYAN:
(*not convinced*) Uh-huh. And she stole this DVD from her
father?

BLAKE:
No. He gave it to her! For her "education." "Don't tell Mom and
I'll bring more."

RYAN:
You're serious?

BLAKE:
He told Tracy when she gets a bit older he's going to take her
out for dinner and everyone will think she's his girlfriend, not
his daughter. He's a total creep. I used to think he was cool. _grey_
area
_of_
paedophilia

RYAN:
How does he treat you?

BLAKE:
You mean, has he ever touched me? No. The whole family is freaky. Tracy's twin sisters kick me and call me HUGO.

RYAN:
What's HUGO?

BLAKE:
Huge Ugly Gay Organism. Because I have a boy's name. Those twins are from Satan. And her mom got hugely fat and just stares at me, doesn't say hi. She's always eating cheap Safeway-brand ice cream, even though they can totally afford Häagen-Dazs.

RYAN:
Do you think Tracy's dad has ... touched the girls?

BLAKE:
Nah. She would tell me. But you should hear what my mom says.

RYAN:
Greta knows?

BLAKE:
Not everything. Mom's a spaz. She took this course and now she thinks she can analyze people's handwriting. She keeps looking at my homework to see if I'm circling my signature or writing at a downwards slant, which would mean I'm depressed. You know, instead of just asking me. Sometimes I write her a note after school like (*writes huge jags in the air, downwards slant*): "I have my piano lesson tonight, Mom." Drives her nuts. Well, one day, she saw some of Tracy's home-work. "Blake, your friend is seriously disturbed! Look at her *J*s!" (*stands*) So, are we done?

RYAN:
Sure.

BLAKE:
  Do you think I'm gay?

RYAN:
  You're a thinker.

BLAKE:
  Are you gay?

RYAN:
  I'm a priest.

BLAKE:
  Good answer.

SCENE SIX

LEAP is primping in front of the mirror. He fixes his hair just so. He's a beautiful, well-built man and extremely well groomed. When trying to put on his tie, he calls for help without thinking.

LEAP:
  Sonja! Can you –

Remembers … stops … slowly pulls off the tie.

MARTHA leads a funeral hymn.

RYAN, wearing his vestments, joins MARTHA and prays over the casket.

LEAP sits alone, away from the casket.

GRETA and BLAKE take turns viewing the body.
BLAKE becomes dizzy and GRETA leads her out
into the garden for some air.

LEAP approaches the casket alone, stares. Speaks
to it.

LEAP:
Thanks a lot.

He closes the lid unceremoniously and heads out.
RYAN watches, then leads the body out. MARTHA
gingerly steps into the garden to see if she can
help.

GRETA instructs BLAKE to put her head between
her knees.

GRETA:
Deep breaths, Blake. It'll pass.

MARTHA:
Cup of tea? There are refreshments ...

GRETA:
I'll get it, thanks. So shocking to see an open casket but then,
five minutes later, we're eating pinwheel sandwiches over the
corpse.

GRETA heads out for tea. BLAKE plucks a blade of } se─mval
grass, splits a hole in the middle of it, and whistles }
through it. MARTHA watches her awkward
innocence.

MARTHA:
Where did you get the name "Blake" anyway? Unusual for
a girl.

BLAKE:
The poet. Single moms get away with murder.

MARTHA:
One of my favourite mystics was a woman who had a man's name – Julian of Norwich. She experienced intense visions of Jesus in a female form.

BLAKE:
Jesus in drag?

MARTHA:
Well ... more like God as a loving mother figure.

BLAKE:
Did she get burned at the stake?

MARTHA:
No. She was an honoured anchoress of the Middle Ages. A misfit. Like you.

BLAKE:
Like me?

MARTHA:
You don't blindly follow the crowd. I think the misfits understand God the best. Most mystical experiences happen when people are in transition between two worlds: when they're in-between young and old; between man and woman. Between alive and dead.

BLAKE:
The song you sang last week, you know, the one the boys laughed at ...?

MARTHA:
Yes?

BLAKE:
They were jerks. I thought you were brave. I like the idea of tasting God. You know, like the song said. Having God that real. Doesn't have to be perverted.

 MARTHA: *mirroring motif*
No. Not at all. People make fun of what they don't understand.

> *MARTHA sighs and pats BLAKE's leg. LEAP enters, captures a bee, sticks the stinger in his elbow, then squishes it.*

LEAP:
Good for the arthritis.

> *MARTHA and BLAKE look at LEAP as if he were weird.*

MARTHA:
I think I'll stick to Lakota.

BLAKE:
Miss Woods, do you ... agree with everything the church says?

MARTHA:
No. I think women should be priests. I think contraceptives should be sanctioned.   *modern. progressive m some ways.*

> *GRETA and RYAN enter at different times, overhearing. GRETA carries a cup of tea for BLAKE and munches a pinwheel sandwich.*

BLAKE:
Yeah, and so much else. I don't know if I can call myself a Catholic.

MARTHA:
Change won't happen if the thinkers leave.

GRETA:
(*interrupts*) Gorgeous day.

MARTHA:
(*continuing her conversation with BLAKE*) You know, the mystics I've been focusing on in worship? Like Hildegard von Bingen? They all challenged doctrine.

> *RYAN picks up a blade of grass, tries to whistle like BLAKE. No luck.*

GRETA:
Leap, you want a coffee? Or are you still "no caffeine"?

LEAP:
I'm fine.

GRETA:
Plate of veggies?

LEAP:
Greta. No.

RYAN:
Church is like marriage. You're not going to find that perfect someone who believes exactly what you believe. So you choose what you can live with. *Parralle]*

GRETA:
Or you can choose to be alone.

LEAP:
Try Russia with all the cathedrals boarded up. You read Bible verses written by hand, little scraps of paper, stuffed in a sock. You pray with Christians in a basement as if you were dealing crack – afraid you'll get busted and rot in jail. You come to Canada – beautiful churches with the doors wide open – cushions for your ass ... and what? Empty.

 Paradox

GRETA:
Because it's old fashioned.

LEAP:
Modern is shit. Easy to complain about everything. The Pope,
abortion. Should gays get married? Let them do what they
want. Just don't do it to me. And let the church be what it is.
Done.

GRETA:
It's not as simple as that.

LEAP:
Am I an idiot?

MARTHA:
We're just saying there are things to question ...

LEAP:
Why question? It's either faith or it isn't. At the end of the day,
I sleep through the night. Do you?

*LEAP leaves, RYAN follows. MARTHA whispers to
RYAN on the way out ...*

MARTHA:
She's special, that one. I love that kid.

Once they're alone, BLAKE squints at GRETA.

BLAKE:
What's with that guy, Mom? Did you go out with him?

GRETA:
Why?

BLAKE:
Well ... you never talk to him. But it seems like you know each
other.

GRETA:
Yes. He left me for Sonja. At a very bad time.

BLAKE whistles through her grass again.

GRETA:
Sometimes I get fed up with church too. But then Father
Ryan gives a thought-provoking mass, the outreach programs
are feeding the homeless downtown, the shelter is bursting
at the seams with women in need, even with government
cutbacks ... but ... mostly, if I think about it, I go to church for
forgiveness.

BLAKE:
Seriously? Doesn't the prayer of contrition make you feel like
shit?

GRETA:
No. I feel like shit because I do shitty things. I don't know
how the Buddhists do it. I could never get by on being a good
person. "Grace over Karma," as Bono says.

BLAKE:
You're not a big sinner, like, serial-killer type.

GRETA:
No. My sins aren't remarkable. They're the little shitty things I
do that keep me from being remarkable.

BLAKE:
Wow. I think we just said "shit," in church, four times.

GRETA:
My lack of virtue is a given, and absolution makes me feel
innocent again. You know? Like when I was little and could
climb up a tree, slide down with the trunk between my legs.
"Hey look, Mommy, this feels good!" (*as mom*) "Greta, leave
that tree alone!"

BLAKE:
(*chuckles*) Uh, splinter, like, ouch.

GRETA:
I used to swim in the lake and not think about duck turd and leeches. I used to think Velveeta on hot dogs was good for me.

BLAKE:
So, church ... makes you feel like a kid?

GRETA:
Yeah. It dries me off with a towel, smothers me in Noxzema, and says, "Go now in peace."

BLAKE:
Ooh, generation gap.

> *BLAKE gives her a playful bodycheck and they head out.*

SCENE SEVEN

> *LEAP is working in the church courtyard while MARTHA practises music in the sanctuary. He wears his tool belt but not his shirt: he's hot. And yes, he's hot. GRETA approaches him with a casserole.*

GRETA:
I brought you lunch. I hope you like kale. It's an antioxidant, good for purifying ... the body. The blood. It's good for the body ... overall.

LEAP:
I ate too much cabbage in Russia.

GRETA:
You can pick it out.

LEAP:

No. It's good to eat things you don't like sometimes.

GRETA:

I just ... didn't want you to starve.

LEAP:

Starve? You should see my garden. I grew a zucchini as long as my leg.

GRETA:

Okay.

LEAP:

I've always made my own meals, not Sonja. Women these days don't know how to cook. No wonder men miss their mothers. You seeing that guy still ...?

GRETA:

Elliott.

LEAP:

He's not right for you.

GRETA:

Why not?

LEAP:

He's dainty. A man should never go out with a woman who weighs more than him.

GRETA:

I don't!

> LEAP *suddenly picks her up, assesses her weight,*
> *then drops her again.*

LEAP:

Yes, you do.

GRETA:

For your information, Elliott is smart, good looking, and the best lover I've ever had.

LEAP stops to focus on her for the first time. Walks towards her a bit, knowing the effect.

LEAP:

Liar.

GRETA:

You don't know the half of me.

LEAP:

I know you well enough to know you're trying to get in my pants and my wife isn't dead a week.

GRETA:

What?! That's not at all why I'm here!

LEAP:

Well, what else do you want? Gardening tips?! You don't speak to me for fifteen years and now suddenly you're Betty Crocker?

GRETA:

Maybe I care?! (*shoves the casserole at him*) I don't know why I bother. The one I should feel sorry for is Sonja having been married to you for so long. It takes more than a six-pack and a bag of meat to please a woman. Enjoy the casserole.

GRETA storms out. LEAP yells after her.

LEAP:

I don't want your sour cabbage! My wife was a very happy woman! Very satisfied! Lots of pleasure! Lots! Screaming! All the time!

*MARTHA's music stops abruptly and she pokes
her head around the corner.*

MARTHA:
Everything all right?

LEAP:
Fine!

*LEAP is suddenly aware he shouted that down the
block. He slams down the casserole, angrily.*

LEAP:
Bitch.

*MARTHA is startled and darts inside again.
GRETA returns to LEAP, resolute, dragging
BLAKE, pulling her headphones off.*

GRETA:
Please, just ... take those things off for a minute!

BLAKE:
What? Why?!

GRETA:
I told you, it's important.

BLAKE:
Easy with that!

GRETA:
Listen, you two. (*to LEAP*) There's no easy way to say this ... I
meant to tell you every birthday, every milestone ... but you
said you didn't want kids. Blake's a teenager now and she
deserves to know. (*to BLAKE*) Blake, Filipp Feodorovich is your
biological father. (*to LEAP*) Leap, Blake is your daughter.

So bad!

BLAKE:
  What?!

LEAP:
  No. You met someone in Montreal ...

GRETA:
  She's fifteen. Born July 23. You do the math.

BLAKE:
  All my life I grew up with him right here? Sitting in the church
  pew next to me?! You should have told me!

GRETA:
  I thought it would be better to have no dad than a dad who
  didn't want you.

  BLAKE is crushed.

  Protecting kid?

GRETA:
  Blake ... I didn't mean ...

  *BLAKE runs off, GRETA despairs. LEAP sits down,
  very quiet, struck.*

GRETA:
  (*calls out*) What was I supposed to do? (*to LEAP*) You dumped
  me for Sonja ... and you were engaged before I was done my
  first trimester. You must have wondered.

LEAP:
  No.

GRETA:
  The eyes?

LEAP:
  No.

38

GRETA:
I thought that now you are alone ... you might want to have family. She's a great kid. And I think she needs you.

LEAP:
Just ... get out.

GRETA:
I'm sorry.

LEAP:
Go!

GRETA is frightened off.

RYAN's office. He decides to make a call and picks up the phone.

RYAN:
Hello, Bishop Stephen. It's Father Ryan here, returning your call. (*listens for a while, agitated*) Well, I have stricken the Cherokee prayer from the curriculum as requested, but – (*cut off, listens*) No, prison ministry is on Wednesdays, we can distribute the jackets on Thursday. (*listens even more impatiently*) Well, we could sew labels onto the arms – This Jacket Was Donated by Roman Catholics – or hand out Mary-Was-a-Virgin hoodies ... (*listens*) Sorry. I've just been working ninety hours a week as it is ... the point is compassion, right? We don't need to wave our banner and clang cymbals every time we donate. (*listens*) Right. I understand. I think if I just speak to Martha ... she means well ... there's no need to replace her as worship leader. (*listens*) Yes. Good Catholics. And I'm aware that they're major contributors ... (*listens*) Thank you, Bishop Stephen. God bless.

RYAN hangs up the phone, heavy sigh.

RYAN:
Poverty, chastity, obedience ... politics.

GRETA pops her head through the door.

GRETA:
Hey.

RYAN:
Hey.

Long moment. Neither of them knows what to say.

GRETA:
I'm sorry. I am too much. All the time. Too much. *How*

RYAN:
Greta. (*pause*) All the time ... I feel I am not enough. *gays feel?*

GRETA leaves.

BLAKE, alone, whispers angrily to the sky.

BLAKE:
If you want me to believe in you then show yourself to me.
Unless it's all bullshit, show yourself! Please ...

*She closes her eyes, waits, gasps, sits very still,
sinks to her knees listening, sensing a presence,
tasting something in her mouth. She answers.*

BLAKE:
Yes ... Hi ... Hi. (*laughs, incredulous*) Thank you ... (*listens for a while*) Thank you ...

She stays in a position of prayer. Great comfort expands into joy. Then she nods and starts to write everything she hears in her journal. She writes furiously. She writes all of it. Then she laughs and slaps her journal closed. Triumphant. Full of wonder. She runs off.

SCENE EIGHT

MARTHA knocks on RYAN's door with two cups of tea and sets them down.

MARTHA:
Lovely job of Sonja's funeral.

RYAN:
Thank you, you too.

MARTHA:
It is so wonderful to have a priest who is such a dynamic speaker. I always hear every word. How was the conference last weekend?

RYAN:
Dry.

MARTHA:
No offence, but I hate it when Father Chang has to fill in for you. Nice fellow, but I can't understand a single word he's saying. What's his accent?!

RYAN:
Well, he's originally from China but he learned English from Basilian monks in Quebec.

MARTHA:
The lisp doesn't help.

RYAN:
It's amazing how much work piles up over the holidays.

MARTHA:
Oh, I know. Between the new semester starting up at school and serving as worship leader here at the church, I have no social life. Ooh, cookies!

> *MARTHA bustles out for cookies she forgot. RYAN sips his tea.*

> *GRETA approaches LEAP carefully. She has a stack of papers.*

GRETA:
I'm not sure what you wanted. I made copies of baby pictures, school photos ...

LEAP:
How do we know what we want? I'm a butcher with my own heart.

GRETA:
She was always tall for her age. Were you?

LEAP:
No.

GRETA:
Report cards. She's got honours. Not a lot of friends except cousins and a pen pal from Norway.

LEAP:
(*looking at one of the photos*) What's ... with the top hat?

GRETA:
Blake went through a phase where she did a lot of magic shows. Don't bring that up. She's embarrassed now.

LEAP:
She should be. I'll take her shopping.

GRETA:
Look, she's unique. Don't make fun of her.

LEAP:
Why would I make fun of her?

GRETA:
You're already doing it!

LEAP:
I just meant the hat. And why did she cut off her hair? It was so long. Everyone wants blonde hair like that.

GRETA:
She cut it off herself. Believe me, I was horrified. I think she got too much attention. She's a loner but she's great. So different from me. We just got back from camping at the lake. And I shouldn't have been spying but, there she was, all by herself. I saw her take a wet towel, sort of like a paintbrush, and trace around her whole body, leaving her shape on a large rock. Then she watched her outline evaporate. She pulled out a marker and wrote a poem on the rock. When she left I snuck over to read it. It said something about being an image of God, a portrait of water, lifting with the sun. The kid's fifteen.

LEAP:
She's got all her sacraments?

GRETA:

She refused confirmation. She wasn't sure she could commit to being Catholic. I get it. I bring her here because I like the liturgy and the communion every week. Unlike the United Church I was raised in; that's only one step up from a bowling league.

LEAP:

I'll look at all this. It's not the girl's fault we screwed up. You got a family doctor?

GRETA:

Dr. Jody Thomas. I don't know that I "screwed up" anything.

LEAP:

Dental plan?

GRETA:

Elliott's a dentist.

LEAP:

I want to take her to mine.

GRETA:

What's with the teeth? Is she a kid or a horse? Listen, I'm not inviting you to play parent ... I just wanted you to know.

LEAP:

The kid needs a dad. _hasn't till now._

GRETA and LEAP continue their argument. At the same time, BLAKE reads out the poem she wrote as an assignment in religion class at school.

BLAKE:
My "Faces of God" project is based on Revelations 22:13 –

GRETA:
Wow.

BLAKE:
– where God tells John: "I am the Alpha and Omega."

LEAP:
She's getting into fights.

BLAKE:
"The First and the Last."

GRETA:
She's a teenager.

BLAKE:
"The Beginning and the End."

LEAP:
You let her do stupid things.

BLAKE:
If God is the Alpha and Omega, then God is everything in the alphabet.

GRETA:
What stupid things?!

BLAKE:
God is *A* for angry.

LEAP:
This! (*points to pictures*)

BLAKE:
God is *B* for bruise.

GRETA:
She made that costume!

BLAKE:
God is *C* for crazy.

LEAP:
She gets picked on!

GRETA:
Holy shit.

BLAKE:
God is *D* for dangerous.

LEAP:
I'm never going to let my kid be anyone's joke.

BLAKE:
God is *E* for emotional.

GRETA:
She is not a joke!

BLAKE:
God is *F* for failure.

LEAP:
Greta, blue hair? She looks like a Smurf.

BLAKE:
God is *G* for gay.

GRETA:
Oh my God, don't ever talk to her like that.

BLAKE:
God is *H* for holy.

LEAP:
 Maybe somebody should say something!

BLAKE:
 God is *I* for idiot.

GRETA:
 If you tease her I will rip your fucking head off!

BLAKE:
 God is *J* for joy.

LEAP:
 She's fifteen. She can see me if she wants. She can live with me if she wants.

BLAKE:
 God is *K* for kiss.

GRETA:
 Live with you?!

BLAKE:
 God is *L* for laughter.

LEAP:
 You want to go to Toronto; she can stay here and finish school.

BLAKE:
 God is *M* for mother.

GRETA:
 I'm not going anywhere! And you – you're out!

 GRETA grabs the stuff back.

LEAP:
 Give me that!

GRETA:
No!

LEAP:
It's mine!

GRETA:
Nothing is yours! Nothing!

She runs off. LEAP stares after, empty-handed.
Stands there a long time.

BLAKE continues her poem in class. Meanwhile
MARTHA sets a plate of cookies in front of RYAN
and broaches a delicate subject over tea.

MARTHA:
Thanks for meeting with Blake last week.

BLAKE:
God is *N* for night.

MARTHA:
She's acting out in strange ways.

BLAKE:
God is *O* for open wound.

RYAN:
Well, it's that age, right?

BLAKE:
God is *P* for piss.

MARTHA grabs the poem, as though she's
thanking BLAKE at the front of class.

MARTHA:
God is also *P* for provocative. Thank you, Blake.   *ha!,*

BLAKE:
God is *Q* for questions.

MARTHA:
God is *R* for recess.

> *Bell rings, BLAKE is dismissed. MARTHA hands
> RYAN the poem.*

RYAN:
Apple doesn't fall too far from the tree ... you know I've seen
her tag after Greta for years but this was the first time I've had
a chance to really sit down and talk with her. Thank you.

MARTHA:
Usually her poetry is deeply moving. And witty.

RYAN:
There's some beautiful things in here ...

MARTHA:
I think she's just trying to be cool.

RYAN:
It strikes me as earnest. You encouraged her to be a misfit.

MARTHA:
Yes, but led by the Holy Spirit. Not led by a desire to get
attention. This is what happens when a child is neglected –

RYAN:
(*interrupts*) What?! Greta's a very loving mother.

MARTHA:
You think everything Greta does is great.

Forbidden relationship
R & M.

49

RYAN:
What do you mean by that?

MARTHA:
She's hardly ever home. She's either in Toronto or she's working overtime at the shelter. No dad around. And on top of that, Blake's best friend is suddenly spending all of her time with the boys. Tracy will be lucky if she makes it through high school without getting pregnant. If Blake is transferring her sexual energy towards the female, it's out of loneliness. Why can't she still be a child? She's only fifteen. And she's precious. Don't you just wish you could snap them up sometimes? Take them home?

> MARTHA sips the last of her tea and starts clearing the dishes. RYAN takes the last cookie and reads.

RYAN:
Martha, before you go, there's something that's come up.

MARTHA:
(*sighs, knowingly*) Don't tell me.

RYAN:
Some elders went to the bishop, made a fuss, and we've been ordered to end your focus on the mystics.

MARTHA:
Because a pack of horny teenaged boys giggled?! You know what this is really about? Earl Cabbard.

RYAN:
Not just Earl –

MARTHA:
He can't stand it when I stray away from the old traditional hymns. Especially anything written by a woman. Remember when I tried to introduce Taizé chanting?

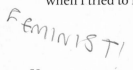
Feminist

50

RYAN:

Martha, you sang a chorus that repeated, "I am a full-grown bride, I want my lover to come, to come, I want my lover to come inside of me ..."

MARTHA:

And next week I'm going to sing "The Flowing Light of the Godhead" by Mechthild of Magdeburg!

RYAN:

No more Godhead!

MARTHA:

Are you making fun of me?

RYAN:

Sorry.

MARTHA:

You want me to edit divinely inspired writings from a canon-ized saint because perverts turn the spiritual into the carnal?

RYAN:

Martha, the sensual mystical is fascinating. I'm a bit envious of Teresa de Ávila and all those lusty nuns, to be honest.

MARTHA:

Lusty?!

RYAN:

Let me rephrase. It's a gift to experience God so ... viscerally. But that said, some worship is public and some is private and best left for one's "prayer closet," as they say ... you don't see me preaching from the Song of Solomon.

MARTHA:

If I was Rebecca singing this song: eighteen, my pert virginal breasts heaving ... Earl would be just fine. It's because I'm an older woman. It isn't proper because I'm old.

(handwritten margin notes: "least sexual is ?c", "parallel between her Scripture & light being perceived as perverted", "gay connotations", "Church trope for straddling private/public fence", "AGEISM.")

> MARTHA *meekly, tearfully, takes the tea tray and heads out with it. RYAN calls out after her.*

RYAN:
> Martha ... Martha ...!

> *He lets her go and rereads the poem.*

> BLAKE *spray-paints a cross to the right of the skirted "girl" symbol on the girls' washroom at school. She hears something and bolts.*

> LEAP *plants a clump of daisies by* SONJA's *grave.*

LEAP:
> You'd think they could mow the lawns, eh? As high as the gravestone. Lazy bastards. (*to RYAN*) Thanks for coming.

RYAN:
> Of course.

LEAP:
> These are from her garden. I don't like daisies. They smell like asparagus piss. But they don't need much water and I'm not coming in every day. She probably thinks I'd let her garden go brown. Wrong. It looks fantastic. All this time she kept complaining we didn't have the right light. Bullshit. All I did was aerate the soil, fertilize. The roses are blooming like crazy. She was like that with everything. No respect for life.

RYAN:
> How's that?

Rebelling

LEAP:
You don't want to hear it, trust me.

RYAN:
I've heard everything, Leap.

LEAP:
She'd say, "I'm tired." Well, why do you think? You don't
exercise. "I'm getting fat." You eat like shit and sit on your
ass all day, what do you expect? "Do we have to phone your
mother?" The woman gave birth to me. You want me to ignore
her? "Not tonight, honey." So you read your stupid book until
two in the morning. Read your fake life and shut out the real
one. I don't know what her problem was. I'm not a fat pig like
a lot of men my age. I'm fit, I'm clean, I'm more than enough
– you know what I mean ... and every night I crawl in beside
her like a goddamn Christmas present. And ... nothing.

RYAN:
I think maybe ... Sonja struggled with depression ...

LEAP:
Bullshit doctor's got a name for everything.

RYAN:
Well, the symptoms fit.

LEAP:
You know what I call it? Ungrateful. You date a woman, she's
all nice and done up. Five years of marriage, you need a goddamn weed whacker. Ever notice that women only tell a man
he's lousy in bed after they break up? As if I'm supposed to be
the bullshit mind reader. If she takes a book to bed because
our sex was bad, then it's her own damn fault. She thinks
breakfast is going to taste better if we go to Paris. She says, "I
want something new," so I try something new – it's like I'm a
freak from the circus. She laughs. Never told me once the way
she liked it. She'd say, "Oh, it's good, I'm just quiet." And she'd
lie there ... like a three-dot pancake. (*pause, looks at the grave*) I

53

told her a million times to keep the bee-sting kit with her; I got her that fanny pack. Didn't listen.

RYAN:
You don't think she did it on purpose?

LEAP:
... No.

RYAN:
Good.

LEAP:
But she always took chances. If you don't look after yourself, soon enough, the people around you have to. We have to feel sorry for you, pick up after you, remind you, feed you, bury you, mourn the rest of your life for you. Well, I'm still young. And now I got a kid. Enough of this.

He's done, smacks the dirt off his hands.

SCENE NINE

MARTHA and RYAN meet GRETA and a sheepish BLAKE by the spray-painted door.

GRETA:
Blake, I think you could start by apologizing.

BLAKE:
Sorry.

MARTHA:
(*gently*) Defacing school property is a serious offence.

BLAKE:
I'll clean it off. I promise. I'll pay for it out of my allowance.

MARTHA:
I could suspend you for this.

GRETA:
Please don't. I promise we'll deal with it at home.

MARTHA:
This is so unlike you, Blake. You're one of my star students. I'm curious what you hoped to achieve.

BLAKE:
It's ... it's a kind of prayer.

MARTHA:
No. It isn't.

RYAN studies it.

RYAN:
"She Christ ..." Interesting.

V. Bold to claim God is female.

BLAKE:
She spoke to me.

GRETA:
Who?

BLAKE:
The ... the ... Holy Spirit. The Female Christ. Her! (*points at the spray paint*)

MARTHA:
Well, that's a lot of bull doo-doo.

Blasphemy

BLAKE:
You're the one who told me about the female side of Christ.

MARTHA:
I think you did this to get attention.

BLAKE:
"Our Father" means nothing to me. So, after you told me about the mother side of God, I prayed to her. And this ... feeling came over me ... like when you come out of the shade and don't even know you're cold until the sun hits you? She said she loves me. She said she's proud of me. Just the way I am.

GRETA:
We're all proud of you just the way you are.

MARTHA:
Blake, I believe God speaks to you; that's why I'm being so hard on you. I care. I think you have something precious.

RYAN:
So do I.

MARTHA:
But don't try to pass off graffiti as some radical expression of the feminine divine. I suspect you pray just long enough to get some kind of inspiration that makes you feel evolved –

GRETA:
(*interrupts*) Now wait, you don't know how she prays –

MARTHA:
– and instead of staying in a state of prayer and tapping into deep wisdom you run off with these lazy profundities and use it for selfish grandiosity by being outrageous. *This* (*points*) is not about God. This is about *you*. I've always made myself available to you for theological discussion, or for counselling with Father Ryan, for any support you need. I know you're having trouble at home but, unlike your mother, I believe there's a time for discipline. overstepping

GRETA:
What?!

56

BLAKE:
    If you want to suspend me, then go right ahead. I don't care.
    She told me to do this. The Holy Spirit is going to work through
    me. And nobody, not you, not anybody, can tell me different.

    strong faith

    BLAKE strides away, defiant.

GRETA:
    Blake! (*to MARTHA*) Watch what you say about my parenting,
    Martha, or to hell with this school, I'll put her in Montessori.

    GRETA follows.

MARTHA:
    Well, Father Ryan, you were completely missing from that
    conversation.

RYAN:
    Why am I here?

MARTHA:
    Because she's hearing the voice of God telling her she's doing
    nothing wrong ...!

RYAN:
    I'm happy to continue meeting with her.

MARTHA:
    And this isn't an isolated incident. She's starting to act out in
    all sorts of ways. Her relationship with Tracy is escalating.

RYAN:
    Then why haven't you brought Tracy in to see me?

MARTHA:
    Because Tracy is normal! Aside from being a manipulative
    little bitchie-poo with a wardrobe bigger than Paris Hilton's.

    sister!

    what is normal?
    she sins repeatedly but considered
    less of sinner as not lesbian

*Two scenes overlap for several minutes. GRETA
confronts BLAKE, holding out an empty
jewellery box. MARTHA and RYAN continue their
conversation.*

GRETA:
Why did you act so stupidly?!

MARTHA:
Blake, on the other hand ... stares at Tracy's body all the time –

GRETA:
(*interrupts*) And for that stupid girl?!

MARTHA:
– is too affectionate –

BLAKE:
(*interrupts*) She's not stupid –

MARTHA:
– does anything for her.

GRETA:
Get it back!

MARTHA:
No wonder Tracy feels uncomfortable.

BLAKE:
No.

> *GRETA grabs BLAKE by the arm, shakes her a bit,
> angrily.*

MARTHA:
She gave Tracy an heirloom necklace for her birthday.

*MARTHA leads RYAN off. GRETA and BLAKE
continue their discussion.*

GRETA:
I passed it on to you as a gift!

BLAKE:
Then it's mine and I can do what I want with it!

GRETA:
It was your great-grandmother's! It's more than a hundred
years old! Don't you have any idea how important it is?!

BLAKE:
Who cares if it's old? Tracy's my best friend, that's important!

GRETA:
You give a best friend plastic, glass, amethyst at best, for God's
sake – not a five-thousand-dollar pearl necklace!

BLAKE:
How much?

GRETA:
You heard me. Now, go buy her something else and ask for
your necklace back. Say you didn't know.

BLAKE:
But she loves it.

GRETA:
Yeah, I bet she does.

BLAKE:
I'll pay you back. I'll get a job.

martyr.

GRETA:
That's not the point! This necklace is about family.

BLAKE:
If family is so important, why don't we live in Montreal with everyone else? Why didn't you tell me fifteen years ago I had a father?!

> BLAKE storms off. GRETA joins RYAN
> and MARTHA.

GRETA:
I think Blake feels ... she's in love.

MARTHA:
I believe what the church believes. A homosexual person is made in the image of God. The inclination itself is not a sin ...

GRETA:
She could just be experimenting. She could be bisexual. Why the hell is my daughter's sexuality anybody's business?

MARTHA:
I may be inclined to smother a baby who won't stop scream-ing on the airplane, but I don't do it, do I?

GRETA:
What are you talking about?!

MARTHA:
Blake may be inclined to fall in love with a female but it isn't healthy.

RYAN:
Why? Outliers are natural.

GRETA:
Outlier? What's an outlier?

RYAN:

Say I roll five dice and then add them up. The sum is usually between fifteen and twenty. Every once in a while, I roll all sixes. That would be an outlier. It doesn't mean the dice are broken when you get all sixes.

MARTHA:

Don't play Yahtzee with this girl's life, Father.

GRETA:

Martha, despite the country, the religion, the diet, the parenting skills ... there's always a percentage of the population that is gay.

MARTHA:

 There's also a certain percentage of the population born with some deformity.

GRETA:

I can't talk to this woman.

MARTHA:

The church believes it's an anomaly, intrinsically disordered.

GRETA:

Disordered?! I had no idea you were such a redneck. Every time you open your mouth I hear banjo.

RYAN:

I think the church should just stick to the word "anomaly." A pearl is an anomaly, an eclipse, a miracle.

GRETA:

Yes.

RYAN:

Newtonian physics, at its peak, explained the whole known world except for two precious anomalies. They led to the discovery of quantum physics and Einstein's theory of relativity.

MARTHA:
And the A-bomb. Don't try to bamboozle me with your intel-
lect. My dear Father Physics, your personal views are more
Deepak Chopra than Roman Catholic. (*to GRETA*) I know this
is sensitive material, Greta ... but if someone is born blind, an
anomaly, that part of their body is intrinsically disordered. We
don't say, "Oh, that blindness is just fine." No. We say, "You're
blind. You can't see. That must be very hard for you because
I imagine you want to see." So? There's adjustment, there's
compassion, there's certainly no blame on the person born
blind. But who in their right mind is going to say, "Oh, you're
blind! Wonderful! I wish my daughter was blind!" No. We
want them to see. And if they can't ...

GRETA:
Then they hear! Then they feel! Then they understand the
world a different way. It doesn't make them any less!

MARTHA:
It may even make them more! They end up hearing and
feeling sharper than any of us with eyes. Sometimes, I believe,
God gives us obstacles in order to direct us to greatness.

GRETA:
Obstacles?! I'm done with this conversation. Blake's gonna be
here any minute.

RYAN:
We should reschedule another meeting.

MARTHA:
(*more hushed*) Please, let me finish. I think your daughter is
remarkable. It's about 10 percent of the population that is gay.
Yes? Back in ancient times when Moses was setting up God's
ideal society with the ten tribes of Israel –

GRETA:
(*interrupts*) Oh good Lord!

62

MARTHA:

- 10 percent of the population, the tribe of Levi, was chosen by God to be in charge of the temple. And everyone else gave 10 percent of their earnings to the Levites. The temple was everything that served the people spiritually: the priests, the musicians, the artists ... Tell me. Why is it so many people who are gay end up being priests, musicians, and artists ... How many priests in the church are gay? Most of them. Artists who changed the world: Leonardo da Vinci, Walt Whitman, Tchaikovsky.

RYAN:

So, you think ... being gay is a sign of being called to do God's work?

MARTHA:

Yes.

RYAN:

But not all people who do God's work are gay and why do they have to be celibate?

MARTHA:

The same reason you are. So you can be married to God. Saint Paul, a notorious bachelor who suffered from some unnamed affliction, said in I Corinthians: "It is good for a man not to marry." "I wish that all men were as I am." Why? Because it's distracting!

And painful. My love life was a bust. Married at eighteen, largely so I could have sex. He was abusive, cheated on me, and finally left ten years later. That part of my life was a complete write-off. Look at Leap, unhappily married for more than a decade and now unhappily widowed with all his guilt over how lousy that marriage was. And Greta: single mom. Not easy. And if Blake's gay, she only has 10 percent of the population to choose from. Look. We've had 90 percent to choose from and it's been a disaster!

63

Father Ryan, you have the most time and energy to devote to serving the community. Sex is for breeding. And when it isn't for breeding, it is for pleasure. And how much pleasure, honestly, is actually derived from the pursuit of it? Giving up sex is a huge sacrifice. Don't get me wrong.

Father Ryan, I'm sure you know that better than we do. But time is precious and, if sexuality is thwarted, it's for a greater purpose. So the gifted can focus on doing God's work and serving the community as our visionaries, our philosophers, our beauty makers. And that's why Satan works so hard to oppress them.

RYAN:
Martha ... the famous people you mention ... they weren't known to be celibate. Yet they still had time to manage greatness.

Holes in argument

MARTHA:
They all lived in a time when a gay relationship would have been taboo. I imagine they experienced excruciating loneliness. And when they couldn't seek solace in sex, they sought it in the divine, whether they called it that or not. We're talking about a special child here. My plea is for all of us to encourage her towards celibacy and devotion.

GRETA:
Are you trying to make my daughter into a nun?! What Blake does with her body is between her and God. It's none of your business!

MARTHA:
Father Ryan, why won't you support me on this?

RYAN:
Because I don't agree with it.

MARTHA:
It's Biblical.

RYAN:
The Bible preaches against promiscuity, primarily. It's very
logical: don't hurt each other. I believe everyone has a right to
love and intimacy.

MARTHA:
A "right"? Love is a gift, not a right. And I'm not talking about
love and intimacy, I'm talking about sex.

Debate-able

→ church separate these

> *BLAKE enters.*

BLAKE:
I'm tired. I'm hungry. I'm cold. Can we go home now?

GRETA:
Of course we can, baby.

> *GRETA puts her arm around BLAKE and leads
> her out.*

> *MARTHA and RYAN are left alone for a minute.
> MARTHA finds a Bible on his shelf and places it
> gently on his desk.*

MARTHA:
We are called to love. We are not called to accept.

Personal choice

> *MARTHA exits. RYAN picks up the Bible and
> heads out to the church courtyard. Picks a blade of
> grass and blows through it until it whistles.*

SCENE TEN

> *LEAP and GRETA sit down in RYAN's office for
> counselling.*

RYAN:
So … we're here to discuss parenting …?

GRETA:

I'm the one who raised Blake, me. Single-handedly. He can't just waltz in and expect to play the big daddy now.

LEAP:

I would have been there from the start and then Blake would be better off. But, no, you don't put your child first. You put your pride. You robbed me out of revenge. *a let child down.*

GRETA:

You want a baby to raise? Get your own!

RYAN:

Okay ... let's just calm down now.

LEAP:

Bitch.

GRETA:

Ass.

RYAN:

Stop.

GRETA:

I should have never told you.

LEAP:

Father Ryan, what am I going to do with this woman? Now she's in my life for the rest of my life and she's so goddamn annoying.

RYAN:

Leap, Greta can't "be" annoying. You choose to be annoyed.

LEAP:

I choose? Okay. That's one for the books. Do I choose to find her boyfriend, Elliott, annoying too? He's not going to be good

with Blake. The man doesn't know how to grunt. He doesn't
even sneeze fully. ·

[handwritten: masculinity crisis?]

GRETA:
Like an ape?

LEAP:
Like a man.

GRETA:
Ha. This one acts all tough but he uses night cream, for
God's sake.

[handwritten: metrosexual. vain.]

LEAP:
What?!

GRETA:
Look at his manicure.

LEAP:
I get hangnails from gardening!

GRETA:
I'm sure he still grooms. Everywhere. Leaves a mound of curly
fuzz in his bathroom garbage can. First time I saw that, it
scared the hell out of me. I thought it was a gerbil.

LEAP:
You have to shave when you're a bodybuilder ...!

GRETA:
I remember once, we went out for dinner, and he took an
hour: exfoliating, doing his hair. And he gets changed, in the
bathroom.

LEAP:
It has a full-length mirror –

GRETA:

- and then he always steps out of the bathroom all primped
up, steam from the shower billowing around his head like dry
ice. "Ta-dah" ... as though I should be impressed with how
beautiful he looks. "Ta-dah!" And now he wants Blake to grow
up as vain as he is?!

LEAP:

Can't a man have a sense of hygiene?! Elliott doesn't even go
to church!

GRETA:

He's not religious.

LEAP:

Why do you want to have your daughter around a man who
doesn't give a shit about the most important part of you?

GRETA:

I never said he wasn't spiritual.

LEAP:

Oh?

GRETA:

He reads ... Nietzsche.

LEAP:

No wonder Blake feels like she's got to be the man of the
house.   stereotyping   discrim

RYAN:

Let's not get into psychoanalyzing Blake ... Focus on the
good things you can both bring to the table as parents. Greta,
why did you want Leap to know about Blake? What did you
hope for?

GRETA:

We're moving into a new house and he's a great handyman.

LEAP:
So. I can fix the toilet.

GRETA:
No. I mean, it will give her a sense of being taken care of. And he's big. Maybe it would be nice to feel like someone could protect her. She should know her heritage. Give her a sense of pride. I'm sorry I didn't do it sooner. I just didn't want her to meet him and be rejected.

LEAP:
I would never do that.

GRETA:
You did it to me. And I loved you.

RYAN:
And Leap, what do you think Greta offers Blake as a mother?

LEAP:
(*sighs*) Well –

GRETA:
Don't strain yourself.   ha

LEAP:
She's not dumb.

GRETA:
Is that the closest you can get to a compliment?

LEAP:
She's got a big mouth but she can make me laugh.

RYAN:
Yes.

LEAP:
Not a bad figure. For her age.

GRETA:
For the record, Ryan, it wasn't me who mentioned my cleavage.

LEAP:
She works with the poor ... helps women at the shelter. She gives Blake respect.

GRETA:
Thank you.

RYAN:
I agree. She's a remarkable woman in many ways ...

GRETA:
I'm right here ...

RYAN:
You're two of my favourite people. And whether you like it or not, this child joins you together for life. So, it's important to be friendly and have a united front for Blake's sake. Greta, do you respect Leap? Leap, do you cherish Greta?

like marriage vows.
↓
by priest

GRETA:
Of course I respect him.

RYAN:
Really? Because you don't let him finish a sentence, you criticize, you control –

GRETA:
(*interrupts*) Now, just hold on a second –

RYAN:
– you interrupt! I think you're still mad at him and you're constantly judging him.

projecting?

GRETA:
He's a human peacock. That's not a judgment, it's an observation!

LEAP:

He's right, you got issues with men.

GRETA:

Not "got," "have." God. Unbelievable. Yeah, I "have" issues with
men; look at all the years I've wasted on them! I'm educated,
fit, I have a solid career, I'm a responsible citizen, I'm on a
spiritual journey. Where's my equal? Anyone? Anyone? *Preach.*
Maybe Martha is right. Sex is fucked. Here I am trying to have
a conversation with a himbo daddy who wants to change
everything about my daughter and a priest who hides behind
a vow of celibacy instead of admitting his feelings! So glad we
had this little chat.

LEAP:

There you go again, Greta, fifteen years and you're still gutting
every man like a fish. You're trying to raise a child?! You're the
big baby. You deserve to be alone!

GRETA tries to rush out, tearful. RYAN blocks her.

RYAN:

Hold on. Leap, that's a horrible thing to say.

GRETA:

Let me go.

LEAP:

It's a horrible thing to do!

RYAN:

Don't run away.

GRETA:

Can't you see I'm crying?! Let me out!

LEAP:

Go ahead, cry. She always does this!

GRETA tries to push RYAN out of the way,
grappling him. He doesn't budge.

RYAN:
You're not getting away with a dramatic exit. Not in my office.

GRETA:
Move!

LEAP:
It's not my fault your dad was an ass! I met him.

RYAN:
Bursting into tears isn't a Get Out of Jail Free card. *harsh*

GRETA:
Fuck you!

RYAN:
He's right about one thing – grow up!

GRETA and RYAN end up nose to nose, heated.
The energy turns unexpectedly sexual. GRETA
and RYAN instantly split apart, sensing it. GRETA
almost smiles.

GRETA:
Spank.

LEAP:
What the hell ...?

The door opens, BLAKE is behind it, blood on her
face. She's been beat up and dragged through dirt. *gay bashing-*

GRETA:
Blake! My God, what happened?!

END OF ACT ONE

ACT TWO

SCENE ONE

Same as the end of Act One.

LEAP:
   What happened?!

GRETA:
   Blake, what did you do?!   *Blame the victim.*

BLAKE:
   I didn't do anything, Mom!

GRETA:
   Well, something happened! Did you fall off your bike?

BLAKE:
   Mom! You never check your cell!

   *GRETA gasps, digs for her cellphone, and
   turns it on.*

GRETA:
   I'm so sorry, the ringer was off! Did Tracy do this to you?!

BLAKE:
   No, a bunch of boys.

   LEAP grabs his jacket, ready to attack.

LEAP:
   Where are they?!

BLAKE:
   They're in the school parking lot. Red truck. I'm sure they're
   gone by now ...

LEAP dashes off.

RYAN:
I've got a first-aid kit ...

RYAN rifles through his desk.

BLAKE:
Miss Woods called you a million times.

GRETA:
Oh my God.

BLAKE:
I need to talk to Father Ryan. Alone.

GRETA:
I'm your mother. You can talk to me, honey.

BLAKE:
I can't talk to you, you already hate her!

RYAN:
Greta, give us a minute ...

GRETA:
But –

BLAKE:
Go!

GRETA leaves, begrudgingly.

RYAN:
We should call the police.

BLAKE:
No! Just – wait.

*RYAN closes the door for privacy, but not
all the way.*

RYAN:
I think we should take you to the hospital ...

BLAKE:
(*her nose*) It's not broken. Don't touch it! I'm fine.

*RYAN rips open a disinfectant cloth and kneels
before BLAKE.*

RYAN:
Do you mind if I ...?

*BLAKE shakes her head but indicates it's okay
if he helps. Her tears start to roll. RYAN gently
and respectfully cleans her face with the cloth,
checking for deep cuts, working carefully around
her nose, hoping it isn't broken.*

RYAN:
It's okay. You don't have to talk. Just relax for a minute. You're
safe.

A confession bursts out of BLAKE in hushed tones.

BLAKE:
She told all the mothers!

RYAN:
Who?

BLAKE:
Tracy's mom. She phoned everyone over the weekend and told
them to keep their daughters away from me. I had no idea. I go
to school, nobody will talk to me. I walk into homeroom and
someone has carved "DYKE" into my desk. Down the hallway
Mark trips me, "Watch it, Jennifer, she's staring at your ass."

Mrs. Randell whispers, "You'll get through this." Mr. Schuler says, "I don't want you distracting my math class, you better leave." I throw up in the girls' room. Miss Woods calls me into the principal's office, concerned parents on her phone. She's pulling me out of school.

RYAN:
Martha expelled you?!

BLAKE:
For my own safety, she says. Talked about Catholic boarding schools for the gifted child ... a place where there's more "structure." I ran out of there.

RYAN:
Where'd you go?

BLAKE:
Can't get a hold of Mom, nobody can pick me up, and I don't want to walk home alone. So I lock myself in the girls' can and sit in a stall for three hours, until end of school. But then basketball practice and other shit, so I wait another three hours, until it's quiet. I peek out, the hallway's empty. I grab my backpack and I run like hell for the nearest door. Mistake. I'm right under the exit light by the ice rink and a bunch of grade twelve hockey guys are hanging around the parking lot. "Isn't that the little dyke from grade nine?" All I can think is, "Cut across the field, they can't follow with their cars." So I start running; they run right after me. No cars coming, they circle around, push me back and forth until I fall. Then they start dragging me across the sidewalk, back towards the field, when a car drives by and slows down. A guy rolls down his window, "What's going on?" They take off. I run all the way here.

RYAN:
Thank God. How's your leg?

RYAN pulls out a roll of bandage and ointment

*from the first-aid kit while BLAKE folds up her
bloody pants.*

BLAKE:
They dragged me through gravel. (*winces in pain*) Little stones
are still in there. Deep.

RYAN:
We have to clean them out or it's going to get infected. You
want to do it?

> *BLAKE shakes her head and turns away, but
> indicates he should do it. RYAN carefully attends
> to her wounded knees.*

RYAN:
This is going to sting a bit. Sorry.

BLAKE:
It's okay. I can handle it.

RYAN:
I can't believe the principal didn't give you a chaperone home.

BLAKE:
I hid out.

RYAN:
You wouldn't have hid if you knew you were protected. *adult
failure*

BLAKE:
She didn't know I was gonna get beat up.

RYAN:
So ... what prompted Tracy's mom to make all those phone
calls? (*no answer*) You don't have to tell me.

BLAKE:
On Saturday, Tracy sneaks a call to me and tells me to come

over at one in the morning. She wants to make up. So, I get there and she's got the tent set up ... we're hanging out ... and Tracy takes off her pyjama top. Shows me with the flashlight. She rubs her pyjamas across her ... you know ... "See how hard they go?" – I shouldn't tell you this.

RYAN:
Maybe you want to speak to a female counsellor?

BLAKE:
I don't want to talk to a stranger!

RYAN:
Just giving you options.

BLAKE:
You need to understand that Tracy did this too, not just me!

She pulls off my T-shirt and rubs the silk against me. "What if I was a guy?" And she ... she starts ... kissing me there. And I don't know what to do. So I let her.

She asks me to do it to her, and she likes it. I can tell. So I keep doing it. Because it feels ... like it's no big deal.

And she pushes my head down her stomach and ... pulls her pyjama bottoms down. "Do it down there, just to see, like they do in the video. Like a guy." So ... I don't know what to do. I ... I do it.

She keeps pressing my head down. She's moving her hips ... "Do it gentle, like a girl ..." And she's shaking, you know ... like I know she came, right?

And suddenly a bright light hits my face and Tracy's mom is in the tent. "What are you doing to my daughter?! You freak!" She screams.

I don't know what to say, I'm so damned embarrassed.

Tracy looks at me, scared, "I tried to get her off of me, Mom, but she wouldn't stop. She's bigger than me, I couldn't get away."

Tracy's mom pulls me out of the tent by the hair. "Get out! Get out! Before I call the police!"

I bike home wearing just my pyjamas. My mom doesn't even know I was gone.

RYAN:
Have you heard from Tracy since?

BLAKE:
No.

RYAN:
So, she betrayed you again.

BLAKE:
Her mother would have killed her! She didn't have a choice!

Still protecting her

RYAN:
Yes, she did. Listen, stay home for a few days, for your own safety. And this – (*from inside his desk, pulls out a card with a number on it*) – is a hotline number, you call it anytime you're in trouble or just need advice. Get a cellphone, have it on you at all times, just for now. And you need to tell your mom. Everything.

BLAKE:
God.

RYAN:
Meanwhile, I'll talk to Miss Woods and see what kind of protection we can provide for you at school until this thing blows over. I'll come visit tomorrow, see how you are.

BLAKE:
'Kay. Thanks.

*There's a gentle rap on the door. GRETA enters
with an ice pack.*

GRETA:
Found an ice pack in the freezer ... want it?

BLAKE:
Sure. Gotta pee.

BLAKE takes the ice pack, exits past her mom.

GRETA:
What happened? It wasn't just Tracy ...

RYAN:
It was a group of boys. Greta, I'm worried.

GRETA:
God. I wasn't there to protect her and now she won't talk to
me.

RYAN:
It's not your fault.

GRETA:
Isn't it? Seems like yesterday I was pregnant. So impatient.
From thirty-two weeks on, "You're viable, you've got all your
fingers and toes, let's go!" I just wanted her out. Not realizing:
I'll never be that close to her again. Then, as a baby, "Oh good,
you can sit up on your own, sleep in your own bed, drink
from your own cup! I don't have to hold you all the time ..."
So thrilled when she took her first step ... when she learned to
walk. Away from me.

RYAN:
She's fifteen, Greta. She'll come back.

SCENE TWO

Several actions overlap. MARTHA sings "Dicite"
with longing, practising for Sunday.

(*singing*)

Dicite
Dicite confort
Dicite confortamini
Confortate manus dissolutas
Et genua debilia roborate
Deus vester
Ultionem
Dicite: Pusillanimes
Confortamini, et nolite timere:
ecce Deus vester
Ultionem
Ultionem
Dicite
Dicite confort
Dicite confortamini
Confortamini

RYAN writes a furious letter to the bishop.

LEAP dumps a cardboard box on his step, marks
it for the Diabetes Association, places in it some of
SONJA's clothing. He returns with some shoes. He
dumps them in with the clothes but then stops. He
squats and holds up a shoe. He examines it, how
small it is. Something about the shoe hits LEAP
like a kick to the chest. He finally allows himself to
break and mourn.

GRETA and BLAKE sit together. GRETA is
programming BLAKE's new cellphone. She gives it
to BLAKE. BLAKE crawls into her mom's lap, like
a Great Dane puppy, far too big to be a lapdog.

She is comforted. GRETA runs her fingers through BLAKE's hair.

RYAN holds two copies of the letter in an envelope; he slams one down in front of MARTHA, which stops her short. The other he strides away with. She reads a bit, then yells after him.

MARTHA:
How dare you go over my head!

She grabs the paper, crumples it in her hand, and storms off.

SCENE THREE

LEAP is teaching BLAKE how to throw a left jab, her first boxing lesson.

LEAP:
Remember your stance: shoulder-width apart.

BLAKE:
So ... when did you come to Canada?

LEAP:
When I was twenty-one – elbows in – defected after Worlds boxing tournament – step back with your right foot, heel off the ground. Good. Try again.

She takes another left jab. He rotates her palm.

LEAP:
Rotate the palm, face down at the end of the punch, bring the fist back, fast.

BLAKE:
Do you still have family in Russia?

LEAP:
My brother. Couple of aunts and uncles, getting old – stance.
Always be ready.

She tries again.

BLAKE:
Any freaky diseases I should know about that run
in the family?

LEAP:
Here. Watch my hips. (*jabs repeatedly*) We are related to Saint
Xenia and she was crazy. When her husband died she walked
around in his old clothes; people had to call her by his name
or she wouldn't answer them.

BLAKE:
Freak.

LEAP:
She sold everything they had and gave it to the poor – you see
how you torque clockwise? The power's in the hips.

He lines up her hips, she tries jabbing again.

LEAP:
There we go. Fist back, fist back, fist back! Left jab is the most
important. Then we work up to a three-punch combination.

BLAKE:
You still box?

LEAP:
Just to keep fit. I retired ten years ago – jab to the stomach, jab
to the forehead to knock his head back, then straight for the
chin. Pango! He's down.

She tries to copy him.

BLAKE:
Yeah! The next time Kyle, Rob, and Brian come along
– payback.

LEAP:
Three to one, you better get some goddamn ninjas to back you
up. Lemme talk to these assholes.

BLAKE:
I can handle it.

She does one really good left jab. LEAP smiles.

LEAP:
That'll break a nose. You know, I started boxing at your age –
same reason. I was getting beat up.

BLAKE:
You? Why?

LEAP:
My father raised pigs. The smell, I guess.

LEAP and BLAKE stretch out.

LEAP:
So, you like girls.

BLAKE:
Who told you that?

LEAP:
Lots of my friends are gay. Boxers – you wouldn't believe –
lots. And gays hit on me all the time. I'm built like a god and
I smell like soap. Sometimes I wish I was a fag because men
are easy to understand. They ask for what they want: simple.
Women? Forget it. Goddamn Rubik's cube with a Kleenex box.
(*takes off the gloves*) You like ice cream?

BLAKE:
  It's okay.

LEAP:
  Come on. I got a craving for that rum and raisin.

BLAKE:
  Puke. Ever hear of chocolate?

bonding

  They take off their gloves and head out.

SCENE FOUR

  RYAN is arguing in his office with MARTHA.

RYAN:
  Blake is the one who got beat up, why is she the one getting
  expelled?

MARTHA:
  What am I supposed to do? She isn't safe at school. Tracy's
  mom has been telling everyone Blake sexually attacked Tracy
  in her sleep.

RYAN:
  Bullshit!

MARTHA:
  Probably, but we weren't there.

RYAN:
  No, we weren't!

MARTHA:
  We're lucky Blake's a girl. If she were a boy, there'd be no
  tolerance at all. She'd get slapped with sexual assault. Look, we
  know Blake isn't a sexual predator, but I still have to answer to
  parents who have a right to protect their children.

double standards

women aren't considered as serious a threat

89

RYAN:
Unbelievable.

MARTHA:
The whole thing is awful. I tracked down the boys responsible
and they're suspended too. The bishop has been in direct
contact with me after your scathing report of how I've handled
the situation ... This is for you.

> MARTHA slaps a booklet down in front of RYAN,
> who immediately flips through it.

RYAN:
(reads) "Pastoral Care of Homosexual Persons." I won't teach
Ratzinger's hate literature.

MARTHA:
You won't have to. Bishop Stephen is coming to the school
himself to contain the situation. He's going to speak directly
from the catechism as part of his teaching ministry.

RYAN:
Martha, the catechism calls same-sex couples "depraved,"
it says adopting a child is doing them "violence" ... It's hor-
rendous. What we need to do is launch a major anti-bullying
campaign.

MARTHA:
I can't now! You've involved the bishop. He's breathing down
our necks! He says this is an isolated incident and, if we show
too much support for Blake, it will seem like we're excusing
the sin. He calls you a liberal priest with a homosexual agenda.

RYAN:
My agenda is to see that no child, for any reason, gets the shit
kicked out of them!

MARTHA:
I will call a general assembly and address bullying despite

the bishop. And I will get in trouble for it! When did you stop trusting me to do my job? I guess it's whatever suits your politics. Or maybe whatever suits Greta. It's fascinating how you'll go straight to the bishop for Blake, but you won't stand up for me and my female mystics series.

RYAN:
I battle the bishop all the time on your behalf.

MARTHA:
But when it comes to worship music I have to "keep it to myself" ...!

RYAN:
Yes! You do! Worship isn't designed to be a personal wank!

MARTHA pants, on the verge of tears.

MARTHA:
What happened to you?

RYAN:
That was way out of line on my part ... it's just ... if we lose our prominent donors, then we lose the women's shelter.

MARTHA:
I had so cherished being your friend.

MARTHA leaves RYAN alone. He throws the letter in the garbage.

Cautiously BLAKE enters.

BLAKE:
You wanted to see me?

RYAN:
Yes. Let's walk. I can pretend I'm on the Camino.

BLAKE:
What's that?

RYAN:
It's a pilgrimage through Spain I'd love to do.

BLAKE:
Nice.

RYAN:
Yes. Peace. Nature. And gallons of excellent wine ...

They head towards the church garden.

RYAN:
How are you doing?

BLAKE:
Cool. Mom started home-schooling me. I'm kicking ass in English cuz I don't have to wait for the stupid morons in my class to catch up.

RYAN:
Good. Have you ... heard from any of your friends at school?

BLAKE:
No. Well. Yeah. But I don't go online anymore. People are jerks.

RYAN:
What do you do on weekends for fun?

BLAKE:
Piano. Leap is teaching me how to box, that's cool. Mom and I are choosing paint colours for the house. I like that design stuff.

RYAN:
Blake ... do you actually hear the voice of God?

BLAKE:
Yes.

RYAN:
How do you know it isn't your subconscious connecting to your consciousness?

BLAKE shrugs.

RYAN:
I've never seen a vision, heard a voice, or felt the presence of the Spirit.

BLAKE:
But you're a priest.

RYAN:
I know. But my mind wants proof. Ever since I was a kid. I remember my cousins jumping up and down, shrieking over the Easter baskets magically left by their beds in the morning, filled with chocolate eggs and jellybeans. I would stare down at my loot, smug in my Batman pyjamas, "This didn't come from a rabbit, you idiots. It came from Rexall Drugs."

BLAKE:
You busted their bunny?

RYAN:
I know. I guess I was jealous. I'm sure their candy tasted better than mine because it was paw delivered, carried across meadows with strong buckteeth.

BLAKE:
So, I guess the tooth fairy was out. And Jesus?

RYAN:
Oh yeah. And the vampires.

BLAKE:

That would be an awesome band name though: Jesus and the Vampires.

RYAN:

It was the same experience with physics. My colleague Michael and I were working in the lab in Erlangen before the LHC was built. He could hardly wait to explore the spin statistics of lambda particles, sure that God was behind the design. I was frustrated by his outrageous belief that our universe was created by an unseen creature who exists beyond the four dimensions we comprehend. I became obsessed with the idea that I could prove him wrong. I'd spend twenty hours a day studying. I'd forget to eat. I couldn't sleep. I'd read until I thought my eyes would pour blood. Then around three in the morning, I'd take a break ... wrestle through the back streets of the city to Frau Blue Tango's bar to drink myself into the mystic ...

BLAKE:

Whoa. You were a drinker.

RYAN:

I was a lot of things. But one morning ... hunched over the Grid monitor ... hungover ... I realized ... I didn't want to negate God's existence. That's not what was driving me. Deep down ... I wanted Michael to be right. I wanted his wonder. I wanted that über-intelligent, loving, big parent-in-the-sky to be real. And I had to admit, there was no way I would be able to definitively prove or disprove God in my lifetime. I would drive myself crazy. It's a leap of faith either way. I had to choose.

I decided to believe. It was a cold, dry decision. Nothing spectacular happened. No rejoicing of angels. I just wrote up my letter of resignation and bought a ticket back to Canada. And like a good scientist, to explore faith thoroughly, I decided to specialize. The priesthood wasn't a far cry for me. I was already a shut-in and well acquainted with poverty.

BLAKE:
I thought scientists were loaded.

RYAN:

Nope. Nothing important makes money, Blake. Labs, hospitals,
schools, churches, theatres. They all rely on charity because,
at their heart, they're all charitable. The priesthood has been
a great life. I pray, I counsel, I serve the hurting. I take comfort
knowing I have given, not just received. But I have to admit ...
Secretly, I still yearn for a mystical experience to prove God's
existence. I still hope for the basket of coloured eggs under
the cross. Twenty years and it's never come. Not one vision
of Mary. Not one breath of God on my cheek. Not one fit of
temporal lobe epilepsy. Maybe, like a clumsy lover, I don't
know how to woo God? So ... you must be pretty special. To
get a chance to talk to him. What is it like?

BLAKE:
Well ... the voice isn't me, because it's thoughts I've never had
before. It's definitely an other, you know. Not schizo, but like a
being, like I can feel her, like I can smell her.

RYAN:
Really. And what did she say?

BLAKE:
Well ... She says stuff to me and I ... and I write it down.

*She pulls out her scrappy journal and reads
tentatively.*

She said ...
    I am the Alpha and Omega.
    I am the worm on the road you can squash.
    I am a dead tree.
    I am a skyscraper and the smog that makes the mountains
        look purple.
    I am the snot a man picks out of his nose at the red light on
        his way to work.

I am the dog who rolls in dead birds.
I am the raindrop down the windshield. Your grandfather's
pipe smoke you still smell even though he's dead. The
mosquito that bit you just above your belly button.
I am the ocean that can sweep you under, the ocean that
houses a million treasures.
I am Christ who hung naked from the cross ...
Is there anything that exists without me?
How dare you presume what is holy.
Maybe Jesus can speak through the gospels even though
they were all written hundreds of years after he died.
Maybe dinosaurs were in the Garden of Eden.
And maybe just maybe Mary, like you, was a virgin.

BLAKE closes her journal. They walk.

SCENE FIVE

LEAP is pouring GRETA a shot of vodka.

LEAP:
Blake's still at her piano lesson.

GRETA:
I know. I'm early.

LEAP:
Happy hour at the Feodoroviches'.

LEAP and GRETA clink glasses.

LEAP:
(*cheers*) Budem zdorovy (*To everyone's health*) ...

GRETA:
Budem. I'm sorry. What I said. That was awful.

LEAP:
 Well, me too. I'm a dick.

GRETA:
 Can I ask you something?

LEAP:
 Oh oh.

GRETA:
 Why do men always leave me?

LEAP:
 Let's not fight.

GRETA:
 No, really. I want to know. For Blake's sake.

LEAP:
 You're a bucking bronco. A little bronco in a woman can be
 good – you want to tame her just enough to ride her. But you
 – forget about it.

GRETA:
 Why?

LEAP:
 You don't just buck a man off, you trample over him to make
 him feel stupid; then you kick him in the taint, then you bite
 his ass off, then you piss on him, and then … you kick sand in
 his face.

GRETA:
 I don't mean to be horrible. I just get scared.

LEAP:
 So when you're scared, keep your mouth shut.

GRETA:
Then I'm repressing my emotions.

LEAP:
Good! Emotions are bullshit half the time anyway.

GRETA:
What about being honest?

LEAP:
Let's say we have a fight and I get so mad I want to kick your teeth out. That would be honest. But I don't do it, do I? Of course not! Some things you repress because you're not a goddamn gorilla. Really. I want you to be happy.

He goes to give her a refill.

GRETA:
No more, that's fine. I have to drive and pick up Blake.

She notices a stack of books on the table.

GRETA:
Read much?

LEAP:
They're Sonja's. I tried to give her stuff away. She had this quilt slopped over the dining-room table for years. Who's gonna take an almost-done quilt? So, I got her mother to show me how to stitch it. Finished it myself.

GRETA:
I can't picture you with a needle and thread.

LEAP:
It's not easy, that sewing. You need math. And these books. I was gonna have a garage sale. But with each one I thought, "Why did she read this? Did she like it? Why don't I read? Am I an idiot?" First one was Carol Shields.

GRETA:
Stone Diaries. That's a good one.

LEAP:
Not bad. So I read all the Carol Shields. Then the Robertson Davies.

GRETA:
Wow.

LEAP:
Now I'm getting to know her. Now it's too late. I always put my energy into my body, from boxing. She was an athlete of the brain. She wanted to go to Europe for the past five years; she'd been bugging me. I always said, "No. I like to sleep in my own bed, eat my own food."

> *LEAP goes over to a duffle bag and unzips it. It has six unmatched shoes inside.*

LEAP:
I was going through her clothes. Give them to the Salvation Army. But the shoes ... her little feet.

> *He cradles a black shoe in his hand. The shoes get him.*

LEAP:
She's not going to walk in these anymore and see the places she wanted to see ... because of me.

> *He hands her the black shoe to look at.*

LEAP:
There are ways I could have made her happy. I'll never know. So I'm going to go.

GRETA:
Where?

LEAP:

To Europe. Like she wanted. (*holds up the shoe*) Leave this at the Eiffel Tower.

GRETA:

Nice.

LEAP:

I was thinking to maybe take Blake. Since she's out of school. Stop in Moscow. Would you let her go?

GRETA:

That might just be the perfect thing. (*grabs her keys*)

SCENE SIX

Two actions overlap. RYAN is in his office, going over his homily. His phone rings. MARTHA addresses a mass assembly at school.

RYAN:

Hi, Father Ryan. (*listens*) What?! (*listens*) Your phone is breaking up ... (*listens*) What are you doing by the river?

RYAN starts to pack up his things in a panic.

MARTHA addresses the assembly.

MARTHA:

Nobody should be discriminated against, ever. Nobody should ever be hurt or harassed for any reason.

RYAN:

Did they hurt you?

MARTHA:

As Christians, we should love everybody and treat them with respect.

RYAN:
Did they hurt you?! (*listens*) Which side of the bridge?

MARTHA:
That includes people of different religions, different races, and different sexual orientations.

RYAN:
Hang up and call the police right now and stay on the line with them. Trust me; just do it! Tell the police everything. I'll call your mom. Hold on. I'll be right there. You ... hold on!

RYAN dials and exits.

MARTHA:
We will be discussing this further in religion class and you'll be handed some pamphlets in homeroom that I want you to read over with your parents. If you are being bullied, you have to feel free to come to us and let us know right away before it becomes a problem. You can talk to the guidance counsellor, Father Ryan, or the hotline number on the pamphlet. School should be a safe place, for everyone. Thank you. You're dismissed.

The bell rings, students are heard leaving.

GRETA rushes into LEAP's yard, frantic.

GRETA:
Is she here?

LEAP:
Who?

GRETA:
  Blake. She never showed up for her lesson!

LEAP:
  I dropped her off ...

GRETA:
  She's not there!

  They both race out.

SCENE SEVEN

  BLAKE is knee-deep in the river, soaked in water from the waist down. She's trying to wash her bare legs, nothing underneath her long shirt, she's in shock. She has a phone in one hand, she's trembling, having lost a lot of blood. She falls over. RYAN comes stumbling down the bank, shocked at how seriously she's been hurt. Sirens are heard in the distance, getting closer.

RYAN:
  Blake! What are you doing out here?

BLAKE:
  I ... I was going to meet Tracy, to get my necklace back, but she sent Kyle instead ...

RYAN:
  My God, what did they do to you?

  RYAN props her up, holds her half-in and half-out of the water as she buckles.

BLAKE:
  Brian and Rob pushed me down the riverbank, into the trees ... "Show me a real pearl necklace" ...

RYAN:
Here comes the ambulance. Hold on. Hold on, Blake. Where
are you bleeding from? We have to stop the bleeding ... just ...
come over to the bank ...

BLAKE:
No, I have to ... I need my mom ...

RYAN:
Come on ...

BLAKE:
I can't get it out ...

> She struggles to rise out of his grasp, he grapples
> to hold her, she falls. He holds her head above
> the water.

RYAN:
Get what out?

BLAKE:
It's too far up, they stuck it up with a stick ... I can't ...

> She faints away. Sirens are really close and roar
> to a stop; police and paramedics are coming down
> the bank.

RYAN:
Blake? Blake?!

> RYAN clutches her, keeping her head out of water;
> tries to shake her out of her faint. He cries out
> desperately.

RYAN:
Somebody, help!

> He rocks her cold little body.

SCENE EIGHT

*MARTHA sits down with her songbook. She lets
all the sheet music slip out onto the floor. Eyes
staring out, stunned. She does not pick them up.*

*LEAP wears a grey sweater, pulls the hood over
his head. Grabs a baseball bat. Swings violently
three times, exits.*

*GRETA sits, a pearl necklace in her hand. RYAN
enters and crumples beside her, stunned with
grief. She runs her fingers through his hair the
way a new, unfamiliar mother would.*

GRETA:
When she was a baby, I'd give her a bath every night. And
whenever I'd pick her up with the towel she would wriggle
around, wet and slippery ... I was terrified of dropping her,
smashing her head on the tile. And every single night when I
safely carried her from tub to towel to bed ... I thanked Jesus
she made it alive. She was a real huggy baby and I'd rock her
in my arms until her curls dried.

Keeping her safe was overwhelming ... I thought about how
she could get hurt all the time. But then she got older, stron-
ger, out on her own.

You know kids. They start lipping you off. They lose that milki-
ness. They begin to smell the same time they start to rebel.
They think they're immortal.

And you start to believe them. You start to think, "Who is this
stranger living in my house? This ungrateful little vampire
raiding the fridge?"

Until suddenly I see her all bloody and white and ... that
stillness ... little purple eyelids ... she's so small. The years

disappear, I'm right back beside the bathtub and realize ... I
dropped her.

SCENE NINE

*RYAN is in the middle of making a public
statement on TV. Cameras flash.*

RYAN:
Moral standards set by the church are there for the health
of our society and the protection of innocents. They should
align themselves with the principles set by our Lord Jesus
Christ. But over the centuries, the church has included certain
cultural biases that pose as morals: the subjugation of women,
the imposition on other cultures, the protection of priests who
are sexual offenders, the oppression of the gay community ..."

*GRETA carries BLAKE's signature boots, gives
them to LEAP to add to his bag of SONJA's shoes.
They embrace and go their separate ways.*

RYAN:
We have to admit our model is corrupted. We have to confess,
on occasion, the church has embodied the antithesis of Christ.

*MARTHA carefully, ashamedly, approaches a
listless GRETA.*

MARTHA:
I loved her since kindergarten. When she refused to wear anything but the colour yellow. And those boys ... I have heard
their voices change. Brian walks home with his younger sister
every day, carries her backpack ... Rob is on the honour roll.
Kyle's father owns the tire shop I go to. How could this have
been done by them? I should have ... been there. I should
have ... done more. They still don't know where Tracy is. She
called her parents from a pay phone last week ... somewhere
with traffic ...

GRETA nods, not looking at MARTHA.

MARTHA:
I'm so ... so very sorry ...

GRETA reaches out her hand to MARTHA.
MARTHA is surprised.

GRETA:
I know.

GRETA pulls MARTHA into her, simply kisses her
on the cheek, and sets her free. Like an errant
child. This destroys MARTHA. She stumbles away.

SCENE TEN

RYAN takes off his clerical collar, slowly,
thoughtfully. He sets it on the desk and
contemplates its white, round, incomplete circle.

GRETA pulls a bottle of pills from her pocket.
Shakes them. Shakes them. Shakes them.

MARTHA surprises LEAP as he's packing his bags.

MARTHA:
(*to LEAP*) Brian confessed. Kyle and Rob are being questioned
right now, at the hospital. Apparently a blond man with
an accent, claiming to be a hockey scout, trapped them
in the locker room. Broke their legs with a baseball bat.
All three boys.

LEAP:
No more NHL.

MARTHA:
I told the police I know nothing about this. I'm sure you know

nothing about it either, because you've already left for Europe and can't be reached for a long, long time.

LEAP:
It's hard to leave justice to a God who turns the other cheek.

LEAP dashes out with his backpack.

GRETA swallows the pills. Too many.

MARTHA enters RYAN's office.

MARTHA:
Can't you wait until Easter before you abandon us? Don't you think I'd like to trip the light fantastic to Spain too? But someone needs to lead worship through advent.

RYAN:
Not everyone is disappointed I'm leaving.

MARTHA:
We need a priest, not a political activist!

RYAN:
Those boys will get two years of juvenile, tops!

MARTHA:
It's not about justice! It's about you coming off as a big-shot liberal. Guilt free. Now Greta can't go to the grocery store without a microphone in her face. And the worst part is, in six months, nobody will remember anything about Blake.

RYAN:
What do you want me to do, Martha?

MARTHA:
Stay. Serve the people.

RYAN:
I can't represent the church. Not after this.

MARTHA:
You can't blame the church for what happened to Blake.

RYAN:
All the bishop did was hand us the new catechism.

MARTHA:
You can't trace things back to a single cause. At least the
Vatican acknowledges homosexuality as intrinsic. Most Prot-
estants believe it's a straight person's disease that can be cured.
And if you start blaming the Christians, you have to include
all the other major religions. How about violent video games?
Social media? TV shows with raped and drowned girls fetch-
ingly naked on the coroner's table? What about the school
system, me, you, Leap, Greta? Blake, for being self-destructive?
Blame is endless.

RYAN:
We are so busy defining our beliefs, sharpening debates,
declaring good intentions, we have no time for love. And
children are slipping through our hands. It's not so much what
the church did, Martha. It's what it didn't do. What I didn't do.
I am taking a leave of absence because I have been absent.

*RYAN walks into a hospital room. GRETA is in the
bed. He sits down beside her, gently.*

GRETA:
I chickened out.

RYAN:
Don't ever do that again.

108

RYAN takes her fist, kisses it, opens it gently. A
line of teeth are in her palm.

RYAN:
What's this?

GRETA:
Whenever Blake lost a tooth we'd name it, decide what kind of
dragon it would turn into ... then we'd put it in a ring box with
cookie crumbs ... Small enough for a fairy to carry. These teeth
are all I have left of her body ... Waiting here to bite me.

RYAN: '
Greta. Greta, you must find a way.

GRETA:
I'm a counsellor. I know all about the grief cycle. I can track
myself moving through shock, denial, anger, bargaining,
depression ... but never acceptance. I just cycle back again to
shock, denial, anger, bargaining, depression ... I don't think
we're meant to lose a child and recover. There's no happy
ending to this kind of story. We just exist past the climax and
live out our days in one long fucked-up denouement.

RYAN:
Come with me. To Spain. Walk the Camino.

GRETA:
Why?

RYAN:
Why not? And you are right. I love you.

GRETA:
As a priest or as a man?

RYAN:
Both.

SCENE ELEVEN

MARTHA comes into view with her Bible.

MARTHA:
The Lord be with you.

CONGREGATION:
And also with you.

MARTHA:
As you know, Father Ryan is on a pilgrimage to Santiago and we are blessed to have Father Chang join us for Easter. This tragic season has brought our little community much sorrow and division ... Whenever I am confused, I return to Christ's greatest commandment – a reading from the Holy Gospel according to Matthew 22:37.

CONGREGATION:
Glory to you, Lord.

MARTHA:
"You must love the Lord Your God with all your heart, with all your soul, and with all your mind. This is the greatest and first commandment. The second resembles it: You must love your neighbour as yourself." The Gospel of the Lord.

CONGREGATION:
Praise to you, Lord Jesus Christ.

SCENE TWELVE

RYAN and GRETA are walking the Camino.
Walking. Walking.

Night falls. Sheep rumble past them. They walk
in the dark, lit by the moon. Suddenly voices flood
in. It can't be from the other pilgrims and yet ...

the night is filled with pilgrims: bodies making
up a choir. They seem to take over the sky, the
earth, the trees. Filling the air with music. As
though every living thing surrounding RYAN and
GRETA is a tiny transistor radio momentarily
and miraculously tuning into something mystical:
they sing "Worthy." RYAN does not feel or see this,
but GRETA experiences this mystical moment
deeply, amazed.

CHOIR:

(*singing*)

Laetabitur deserta et invia
Et exultabit solitudo
Et florebit quasi lilium.

(*repeats*)

And just as soon as it happened, it ends. RYAN
and GRETA keep walking. He takes her hand.

THE END

LUCIA FRANGIONE

Award-winning playwright and actress Lucia Frangione has emerged from Canada's independent theatre scene to take her place as an important, young post-feminist voice on the lives of women in the postmodern world, boldly questioning the institutions of family, religion, and sexual iconography. Her accessible and entertaining plays persist in furthering an intelligent female voice in the theatre, utilizing satire as a tool for critical thought, and tackling complex themes with wit and courage.

Frangione is the recipient of the 2006 and 1998 Gordon Armstrong Playwright Awards, and the 2001 Sydney Risk Prize. *Espresso* was nominated for seven Jessie Richardson Awards, toured Western Canada in 2004, and was translated into Polish and performed at Teatr Jeleniogorski in 2007 and Teatr Powszechny in 2011–12. Her twenty-five plays have been developed and produced by theatres such as the Arts Club (*Paradise Garden, Frankie Armitage*), BellaLuna (*FRESCO*), Pacific Theatre (*Leave of Absence, Espresso, Cariboo Magi, Holy Mo*), Chemainus Theatre (*Chickens, Joy Tide, Christmas on the Air*), Ruby Slippers (*MMM*), Fugue Theatre (*Dog Park*), Solo Collective (*Wobbling Madonna*), St. Lawrence Shakespeare Festival (*Maid for a Musket*), Prairie Theatre Exchange (*Groom's Dog, Diamond Willow*), and Alberta Theatre Projects (*Breadmaking*). She has earned several Jessie nominations as a performer and writer, winning the Canadian Actors' Equity Association Stage West National Acting Award in 2003.

She resides in Vancouver and is a member of the Playwrights Guild of Canada.